Grave Humor

Grave Humor

By M.T. Coffin

A PHOTO TOUR OF FUNNY, IRONIC AND RIDICULOUS TOMBSTONES

Cincinnati, Ohio

FAMILY TREE BOOKS

shopfamilytree.com

GRAVE HUMOR. Copyright ©2010 by the editors of *Family Tree Magazine*. Manufactured in China. All rights reserved. No other part of this book may be reproduced in any form or by any electronic or mechanical means including information storage and retrieval systems without permission in writing from the publisher, except by a reviewer, who may quote brief passages in a review. Published by Family Tree Books, an imprint of F+W Media, Inc., 4700 East Galbraith Road, Cincinnati, Ohio 45236. (800) 289-0963. First edition.

For more genealogy resources, visit <shopfamilytree.com>.

14 13 12 11 10   5 4 3 2 1

Distributed in Canada by Fraser Direct
100 Armstrong Avenue
Georgetown, Ontario,
Canada L7G 5S4
Tel: (905) 877-4411

Distributed in Australia by Capricorn Link
P.O. Box 704, Windsor,
NSW 2756 Australia
Tel: (02) 4577-3555

Distributed in the U.K. and Europe by David & Charles
Brunel House, Newton
Abbot, Devon,
TQ12 4PU, England
Tel: (+44) 1626-323200,
Fax: (+44) 1626-323319
E-mail: postmaster@
davidandcharles.co.uk

Library of Congress Cataloging-in-Publication Data
Coffin, M. T.
  Grave humor : a photo tour of funny, ironic, and ridiculous tombstones / by M.T. Coffin ; [edited by Grace Dobush]. -- 1st ed.
    p. cm.
  ISBN-13: 978-1-4403-0885-7
  ISBN-10: 1-4403-0885-3
  1. Epitaphs--Humor. 2. Sepulchral monuments--Pictorial works. I. Dobush, Grace. II. Title.
  PN6231.E69C64 2010
  818'.602--dc22
                    2010020987

fw media

Written by
M.T. Coffin

Illustrations by
Marc McChesney

Edited by
Grace Dobush

Contributions by
Allison Stacy & Diane Haddad

Designed by
Christy Miller

Production coordinated by
Mark Griffin

Table of Contents

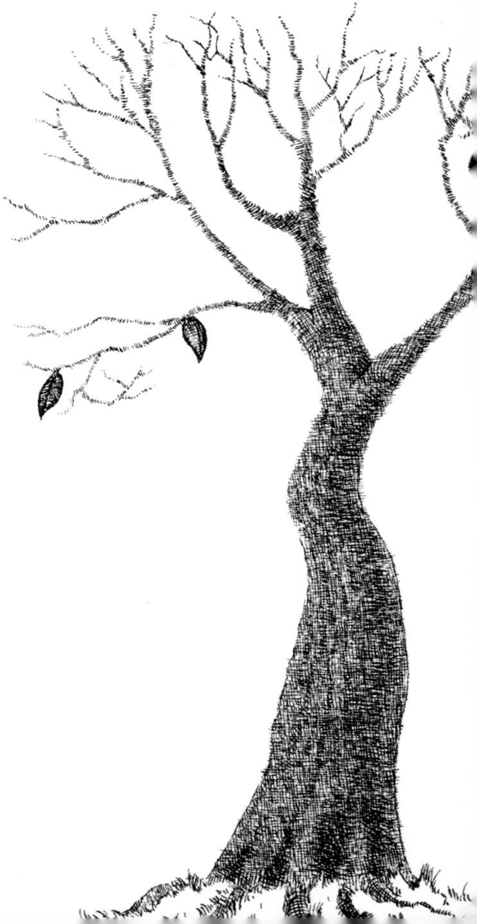

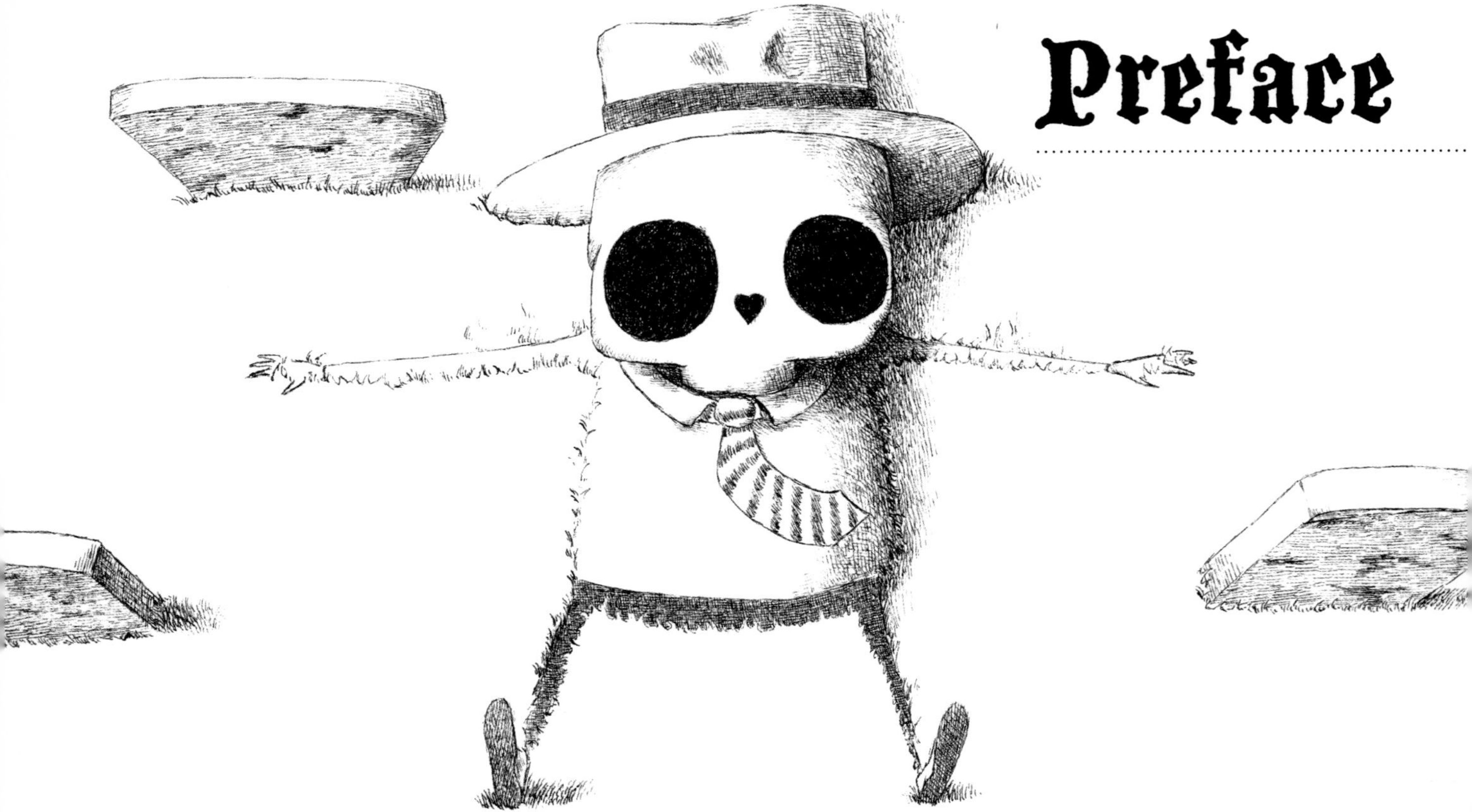

Preface

I was born a **poor miner's son** in **1885**. Though I **died** 28 years later, I still get around. Thankfully I've found a pastime that gives me much comfort in this earthly limbo: **MAKING FUN OF OTHER DEAD PEOPLE** who possess **ludicrous names**.

Ever since I acquired my newfangled Leica camera in 1932, it's been a **DELIGHT** to tromp around the **OVERGROWN GRAVES**, uncovering unfortunate names and **frightening mourners**. Why do I bother **MOCKING THE DECEASED**? Because it's **HILARIOUS**. And because it was this or being strung up in a preparatory school's science classroom.

I hope you **ENJOY MY BOOK** of photographs of dead people's graves. If I hadn't already perished of diphtheria, I would've **died laughing**.

SIGNED, **M.T. Coffin**

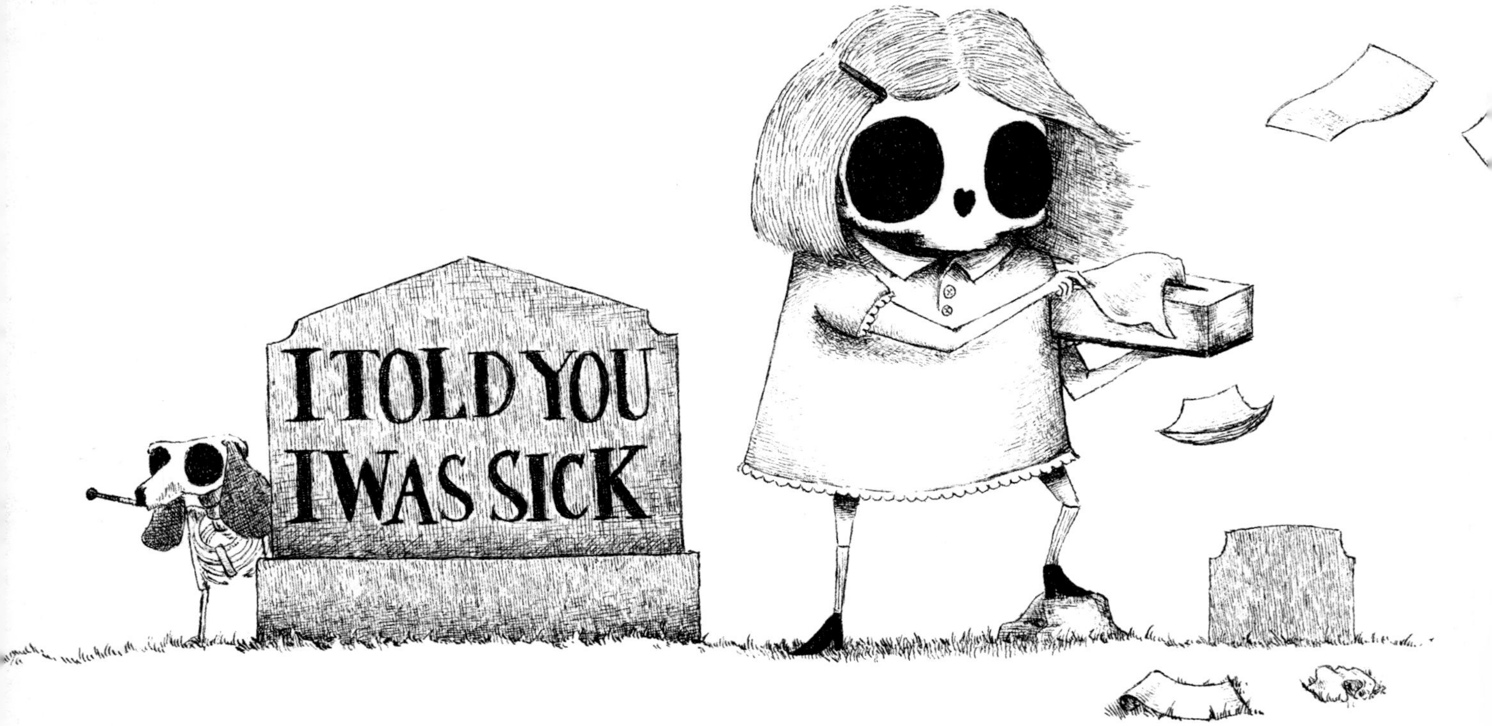
I TOLD YOU
I WAS SICK

THE
LAST
LAUGH

Funny epitaphs caught on film

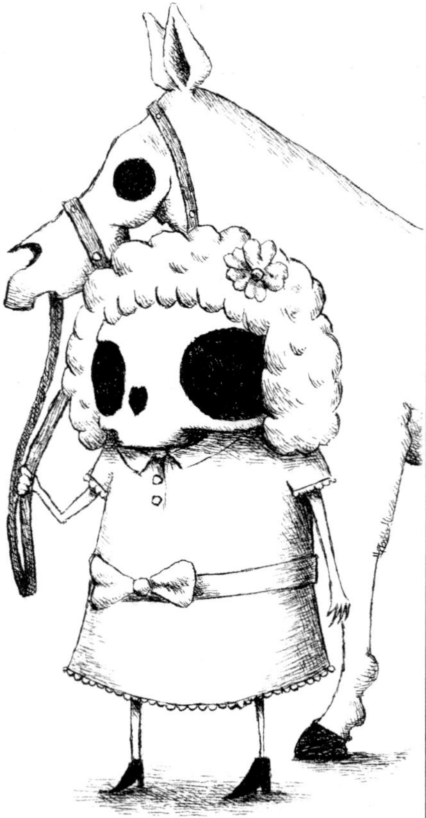

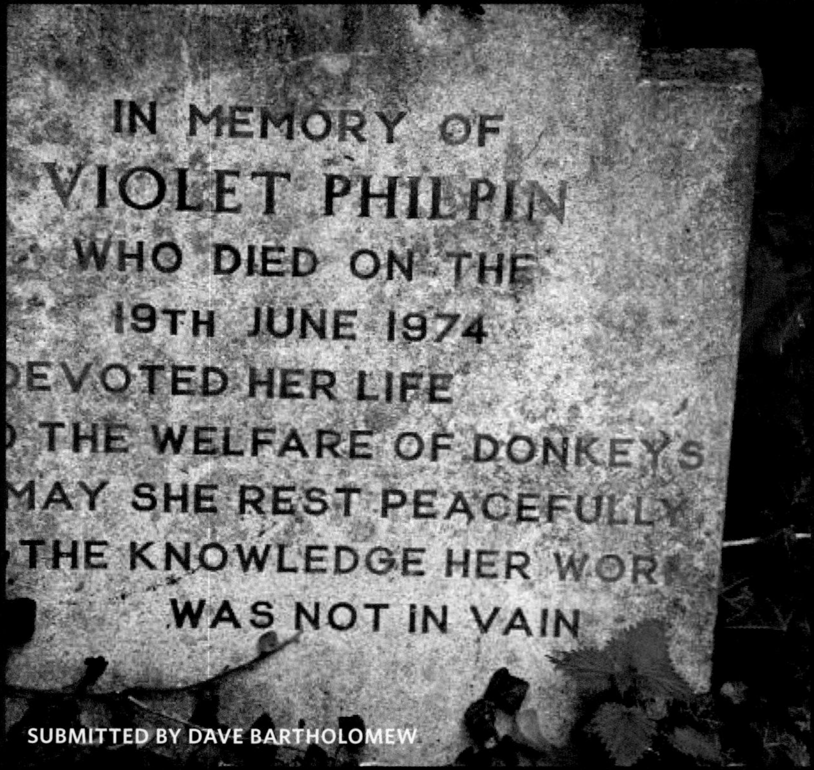
IN MEMORY OF
VIOLET PHILPIN
WHO DIED ON THE
19TH JUNE 1974
EVOTED HER LIFE
THE WELFARE OF DONKEYS
MAY SHE REST PEACEFULLY
THE KNOWLEDGE HER WOR
WAS NOT IN VAIN
SUBMITTED BY DAVE BARTHOLOMEW

Violet finally found a cause she could REALLY get behind.

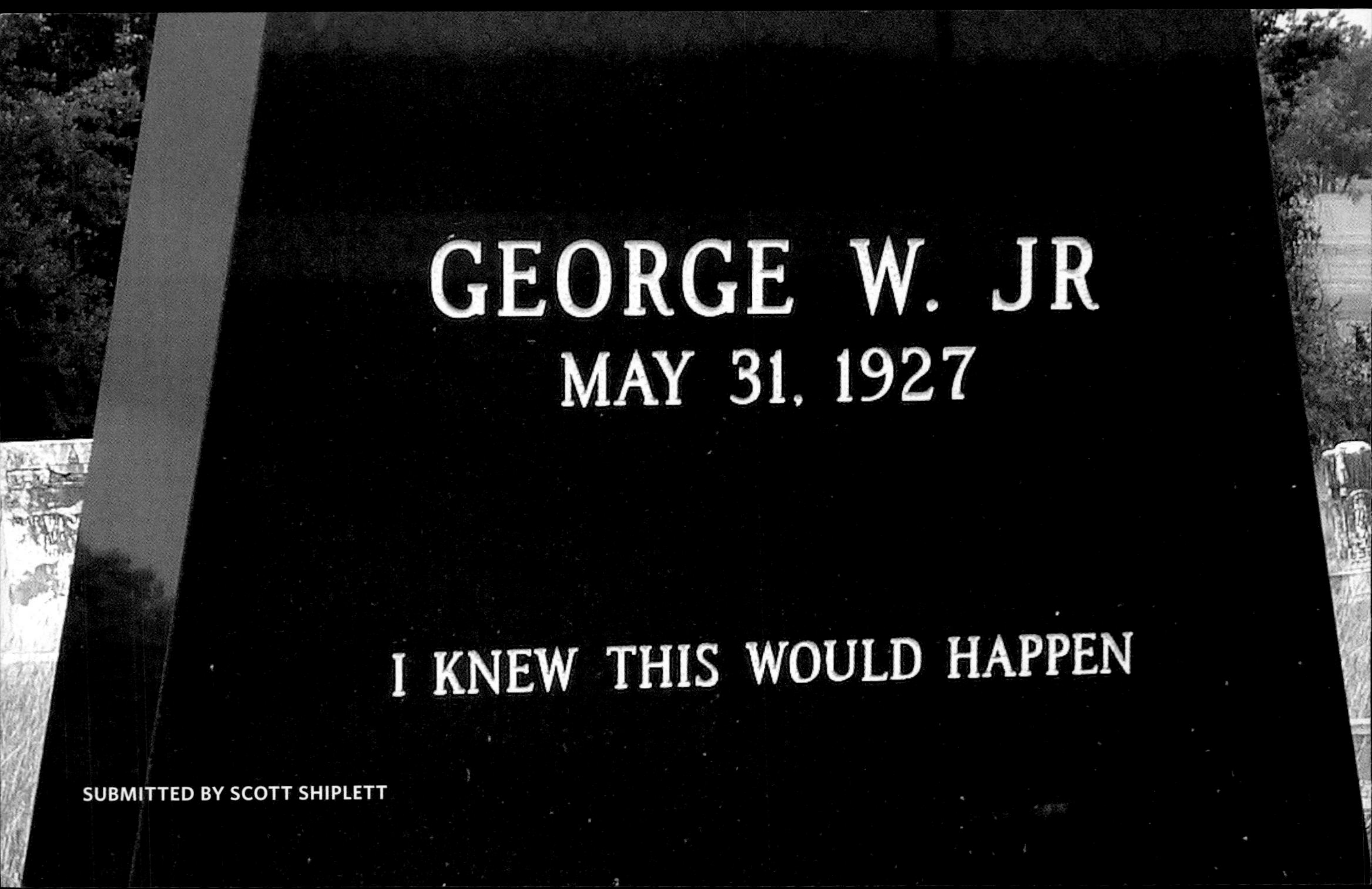
GEORGE W. JR
MAY 31, 1927
I KNEW THIS WOULD HAPPEN

SUBMITTED BY SCOTT SHIPLETT

EVER THE optimist.

SUBMITTED BY KELLY STARR FARRELL

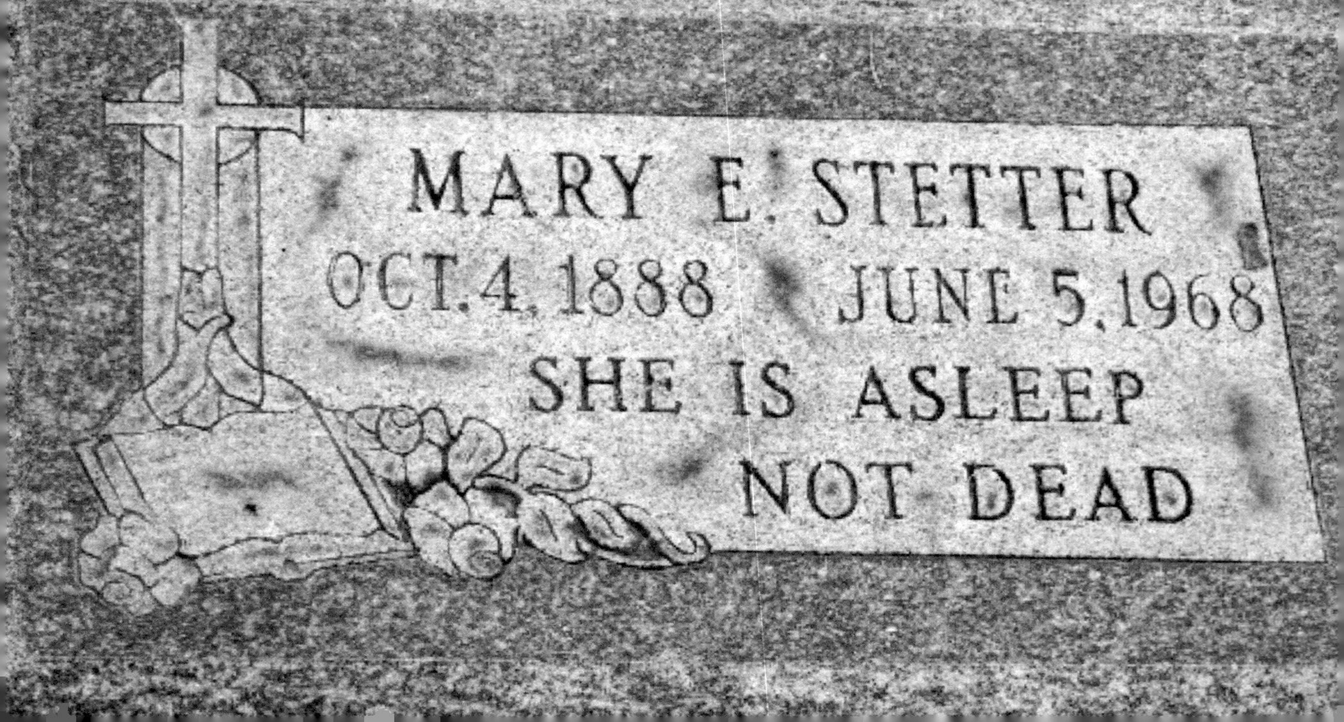
MARY E. STETTER
OCT. 4. 1888 JUNE 5. 1968
SHE IS ASLEEP
NOT DEAD

WAIT!

Somebody let me outta here!

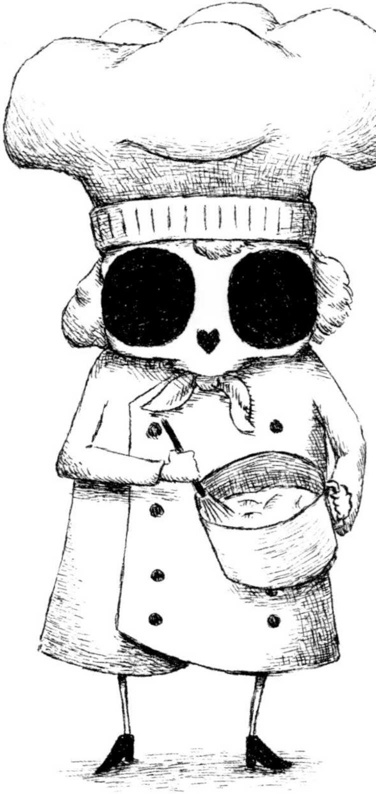

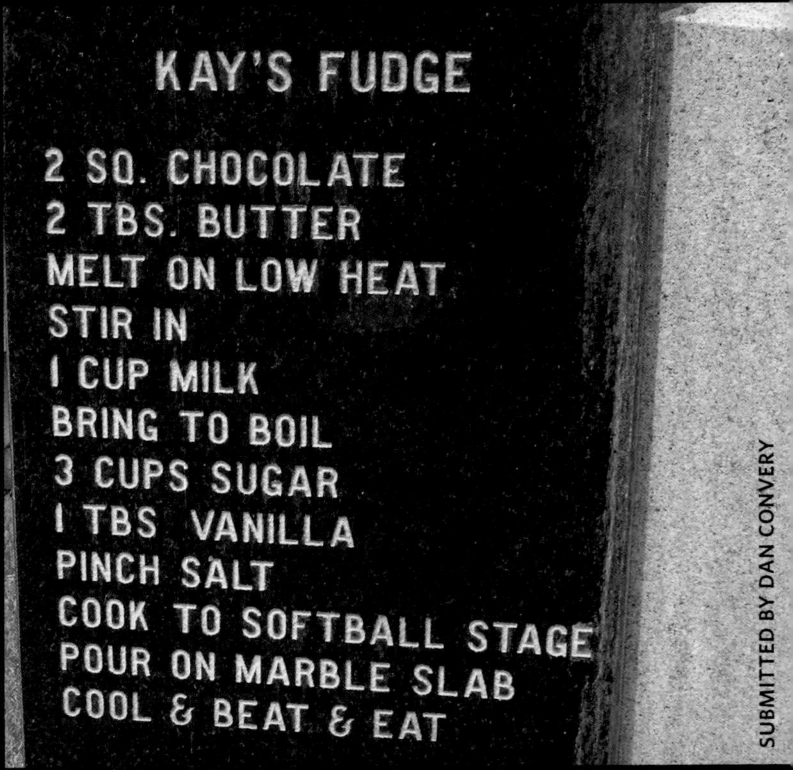
KAY'S FUDGE
2 SQ. CHOCOLATE
2 TBS. BUTTER
MELT ON LOW HEAT
STIR IN
1 CUP MILK
BRING TO BOIL
3 CUPS SUGAR
1 TBS VANILLA
PINCH SALT
COOK TO SOFTBALL STAGE
POUR ON MARBLE SLAB
COOL & BEAT & EAT

SUBMITTED BY DAN CONVERY

HEY,

we know where you can
find a marble slab ...

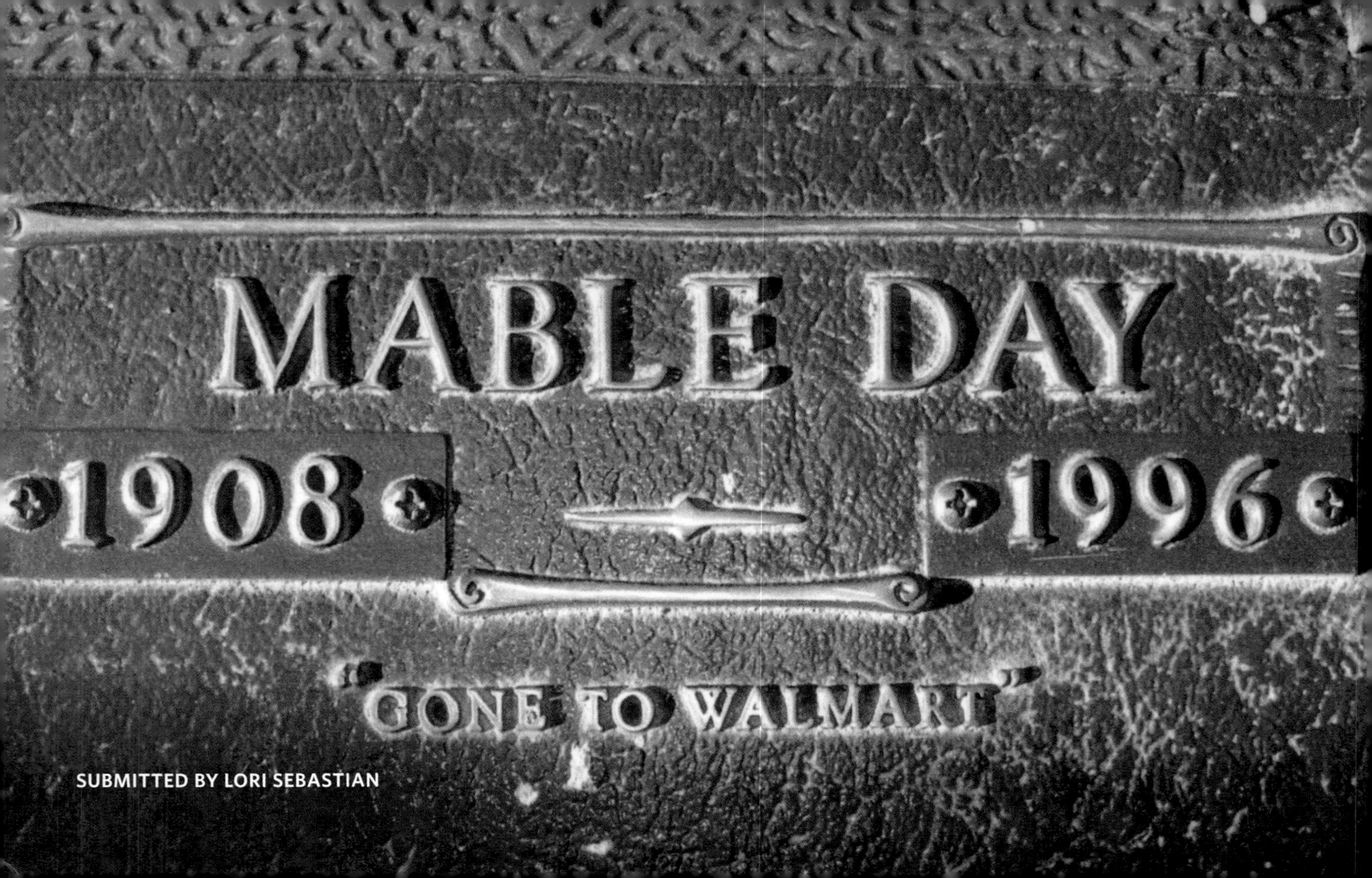
MABLE DAY
1908
1996
"GONE TO WALMART"

SUBMITTED BY LORI SEBASTIAN

So is Mable in heaven or hell?

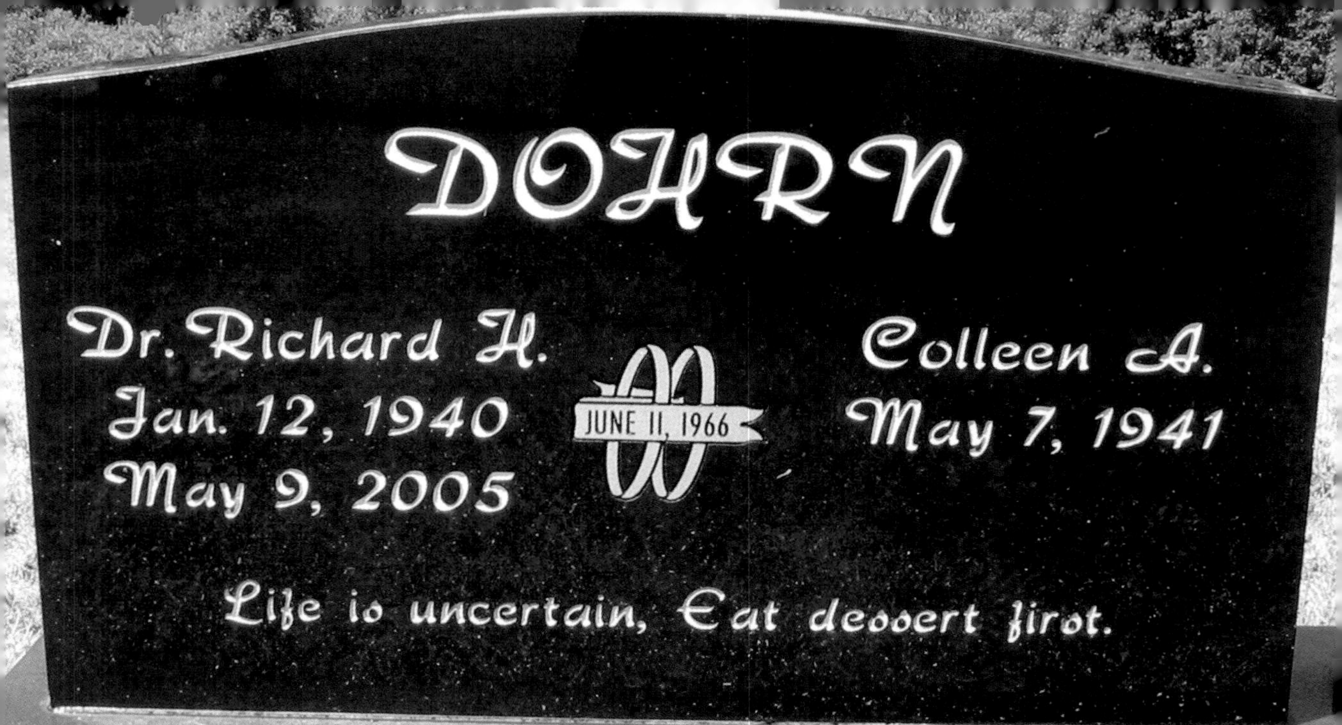
DOHRN
Dr. Richard H.
Jan. 12, 1940
May 9, 2005
JUNE 11, 1966
Colleen A.
May 7, 1941
Life is uncertain, Eat dessert first.
SUBMITTED BY JOHAN MATHIESEN

Ironically,
choking on a cannoli.

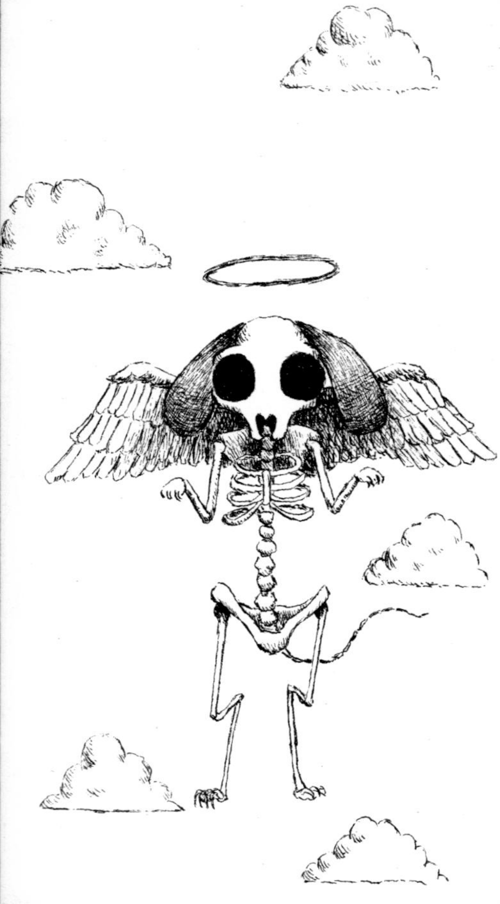

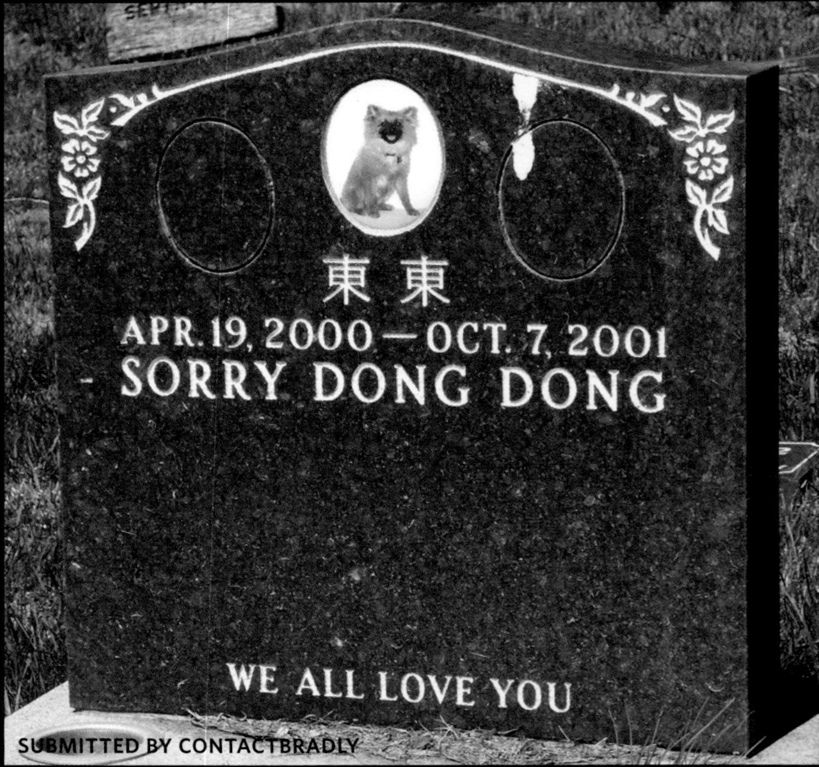
東東
APR. 19, 2000 — OCT. 7, 2001
SORRY DONG DONG
WE ALL LOVE YOU
SUBMITTED BY CONTACTBRADLY

"SORRY"

won't bring him back.

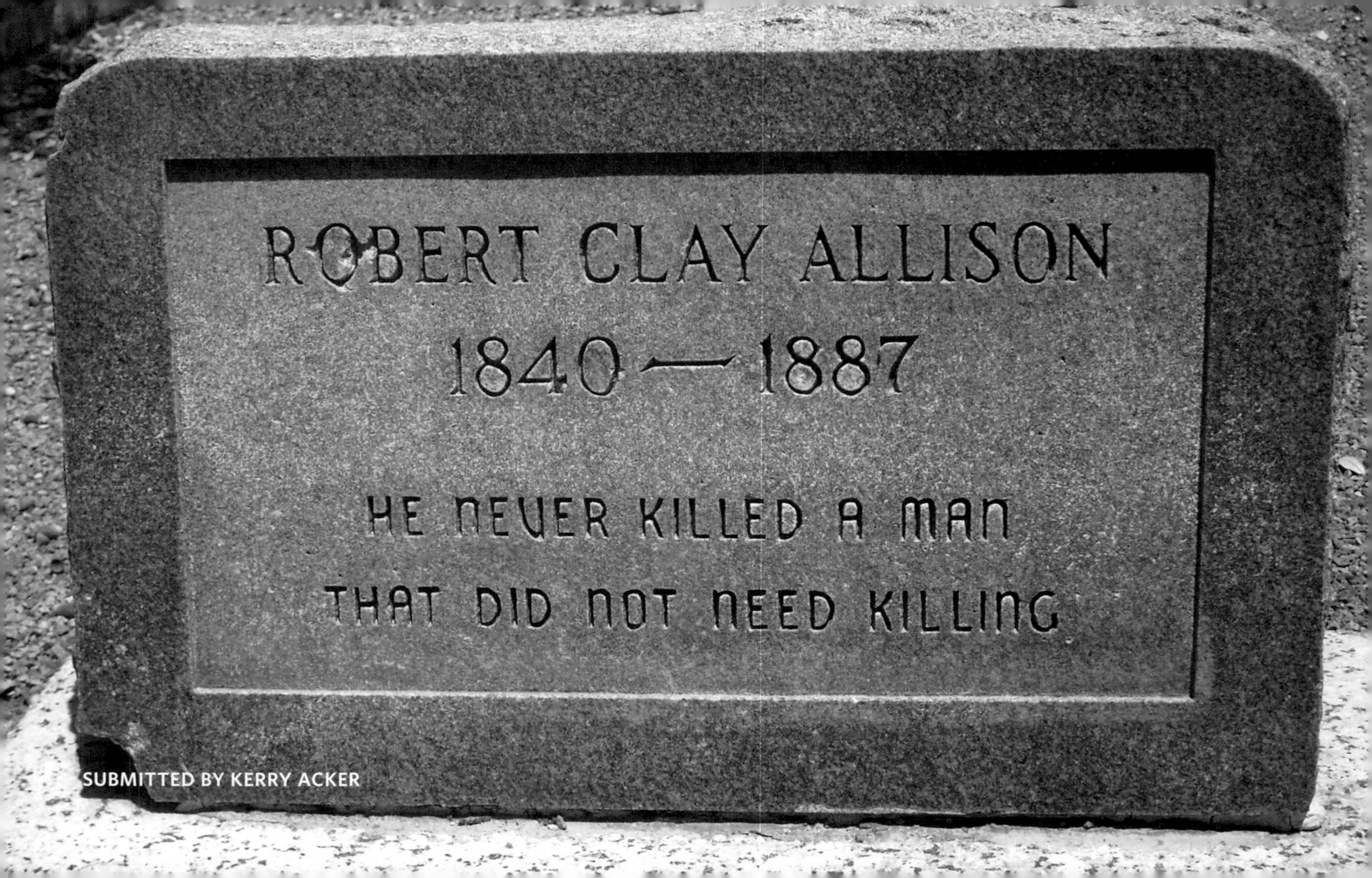
ROBERT CLAY ALLISON
1840 — 1887
HE NEVER KILLED A MAN
THAT DID NOT NEED KILLING

SUBMITTED BY KERRY ACKER

Surely
a judge would admit that as
a plea.

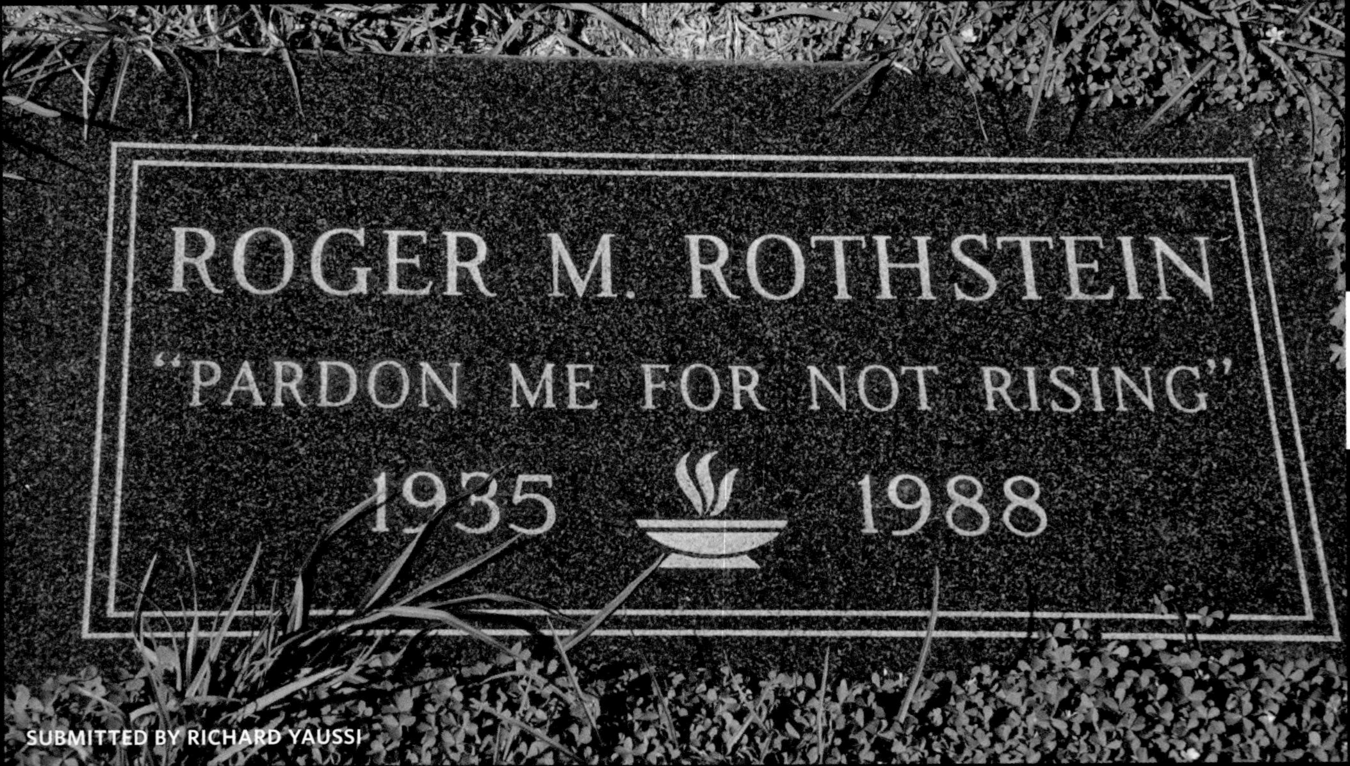
ROGER M. ROTHSTEIN
"PARDON ME FOR NOT RISING"
1935 1988
SUBMITTED BY RICHARD YAUSSI

Ever the gentleman.

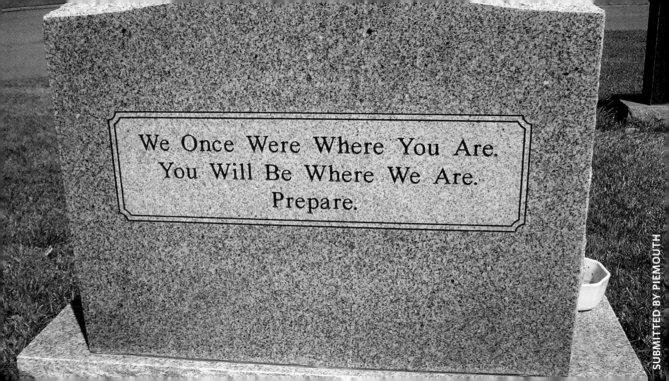

We Once Were Where You Are.
You Will Be Where We Are.
Prepare.

Could you **at least** give us the Google Map?

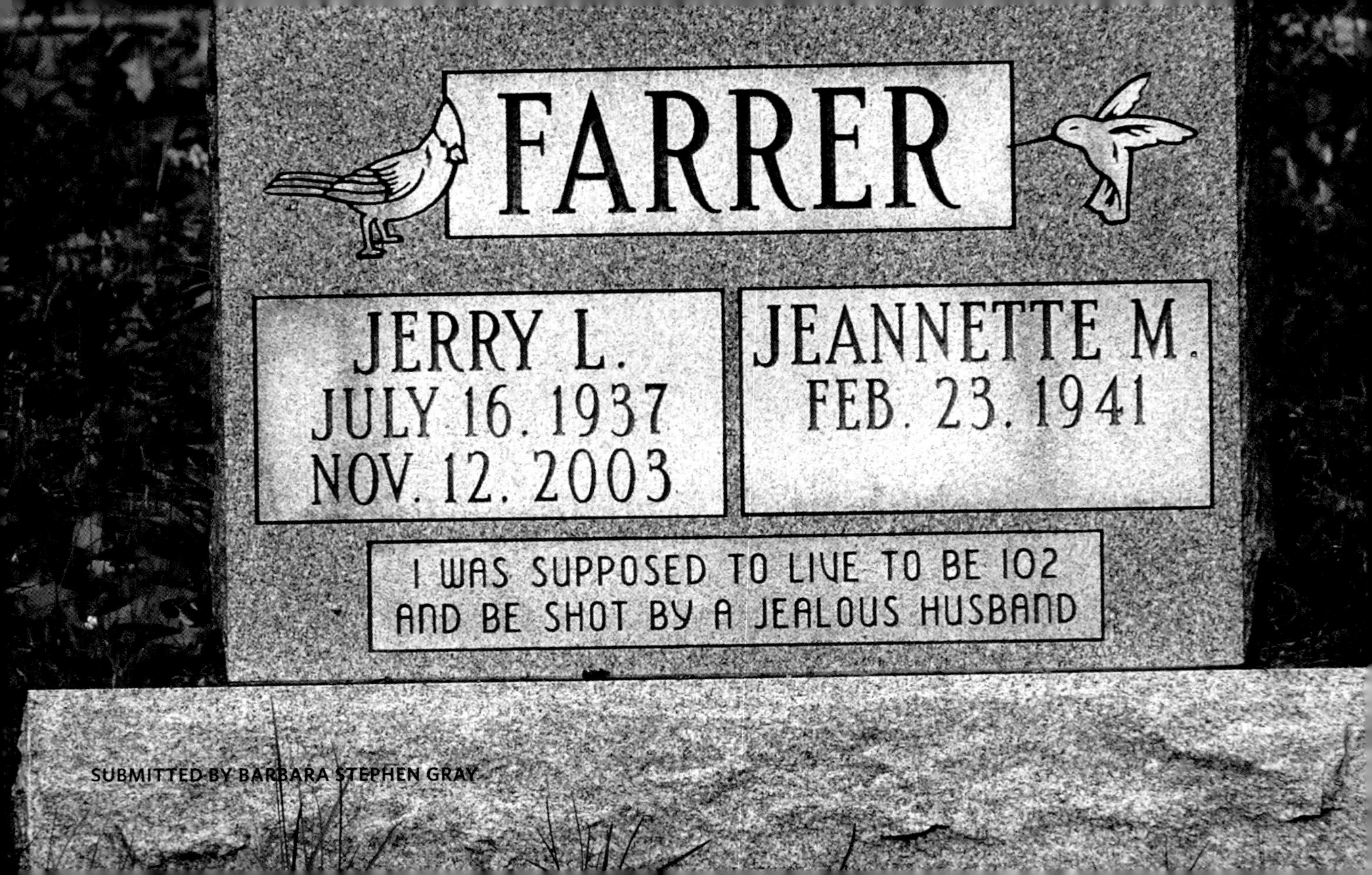
FARRER
JERRY L.
JULY 16. 1937
NOV. 12. 2003
JEANNETTE M.
FEB. 23. 1941
I WAS SUPPOSED TO LIVE TO BE 102
AND BE SHOT BY A JEALOUS HUSBAND

SUBMITTED BY BARBARA STEPHEN GRAY

Jeannette had other ideas.

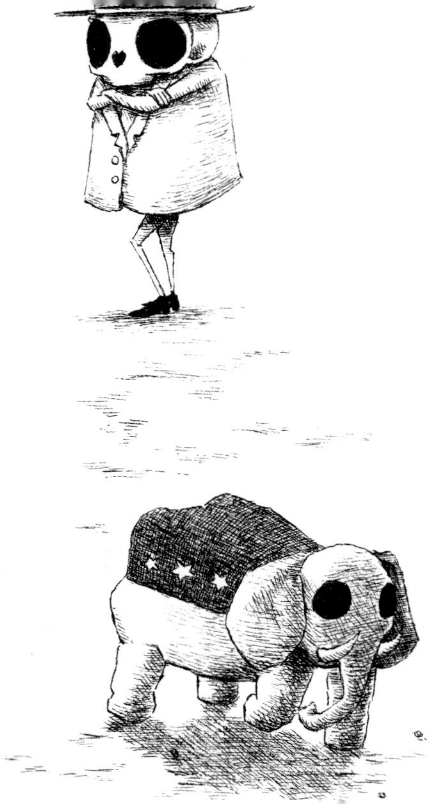

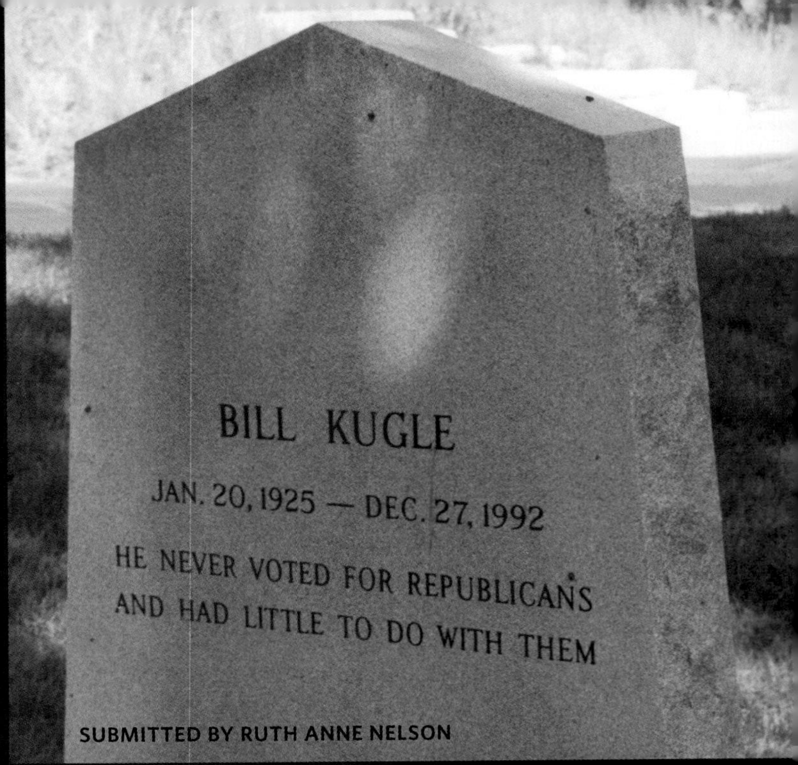
BILL KUGLE
JAN. 20, 1925 — DEC. 27, 1992
HE NEVER VOTED FOR REPUBLICANS
AND HAD LITTLE TO DO WITH THEM

SUBMITTED BY RUTH ANNE NELSON

"I'm Nancy Pelosi and
I approve this message."

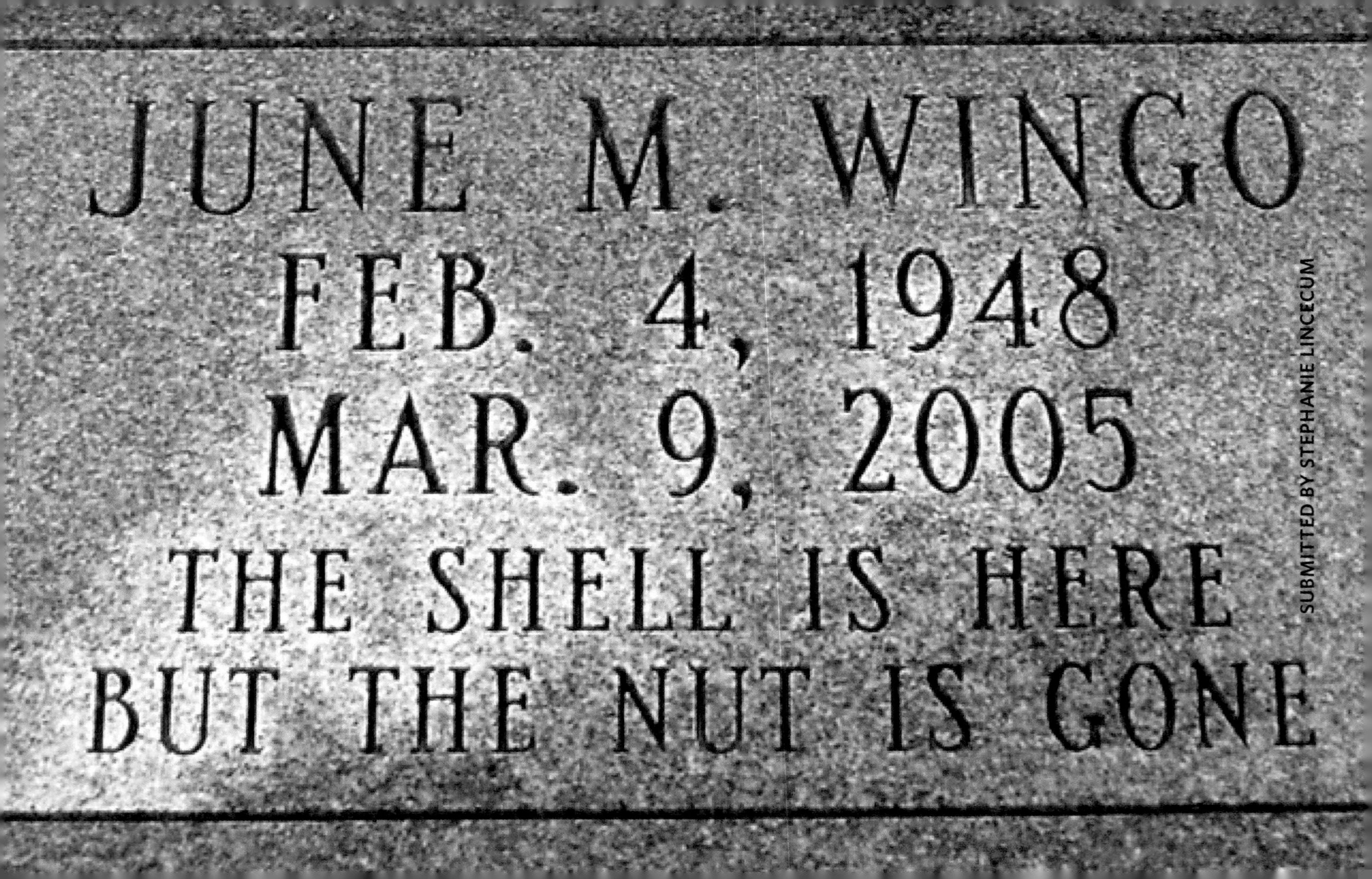
JUNE M. WINGO
FEB. 4, 1948
MAR. 9, 2005
THE SHELL IS HERE
BUT THE NUT IS GONE
SUBMITTED BY STEPHANIE LINCECUM

Damn squirrels.

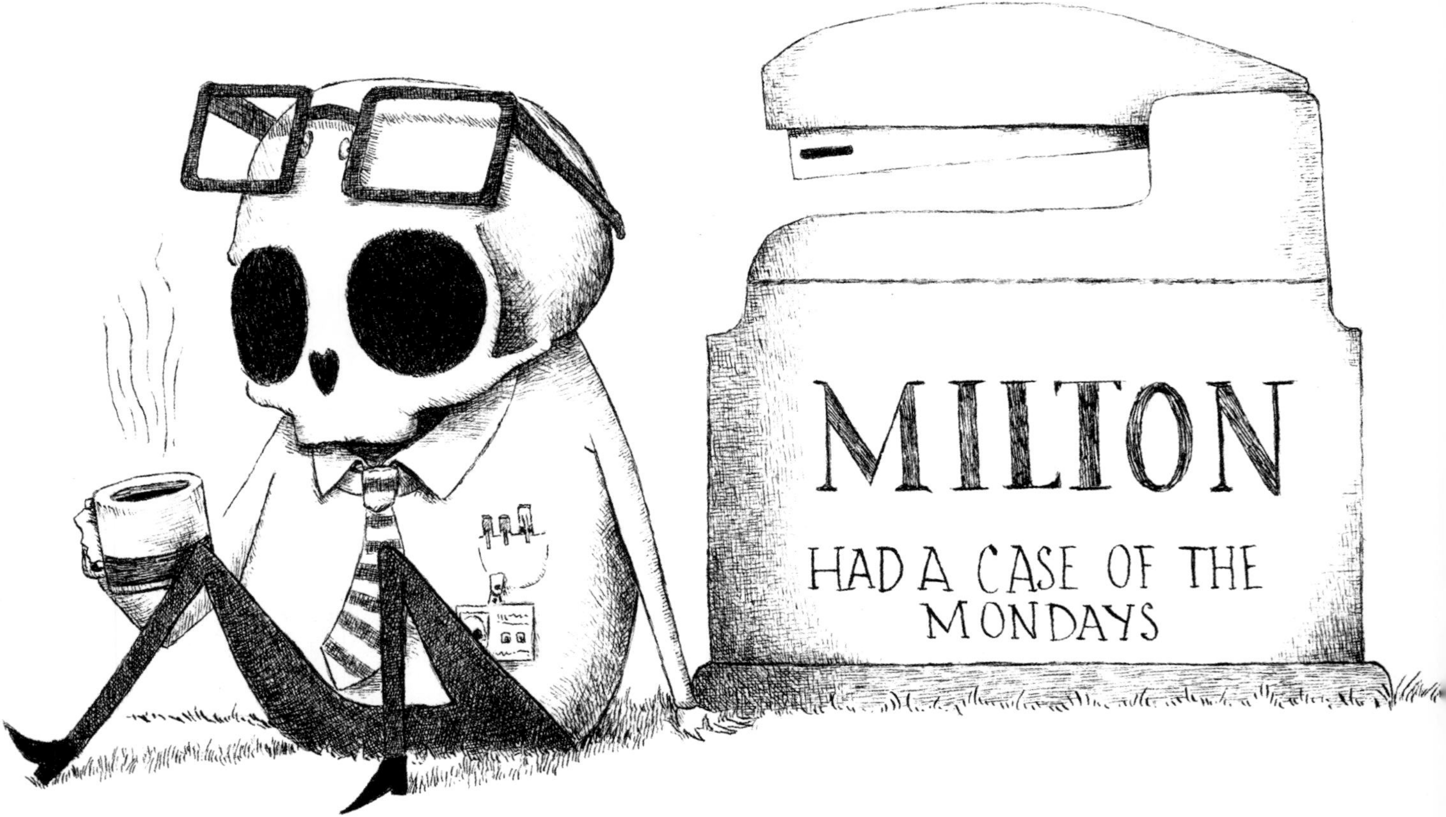
MILTON
HAD A CASE OF THE
MONDAYS

TRUE

TO FORM

Snapshots of humorous and
oddly designed headstones

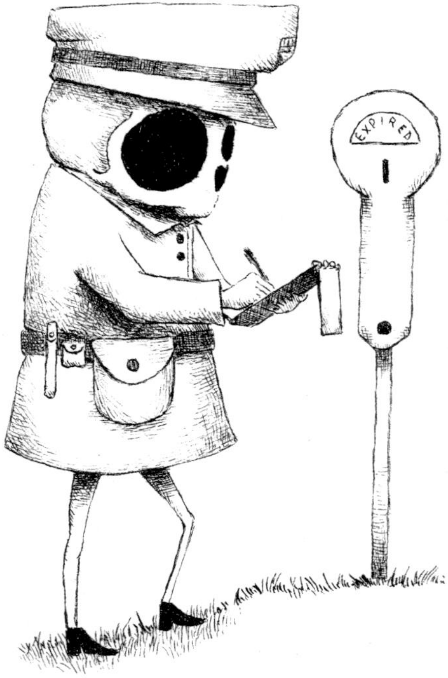

EXPIRED

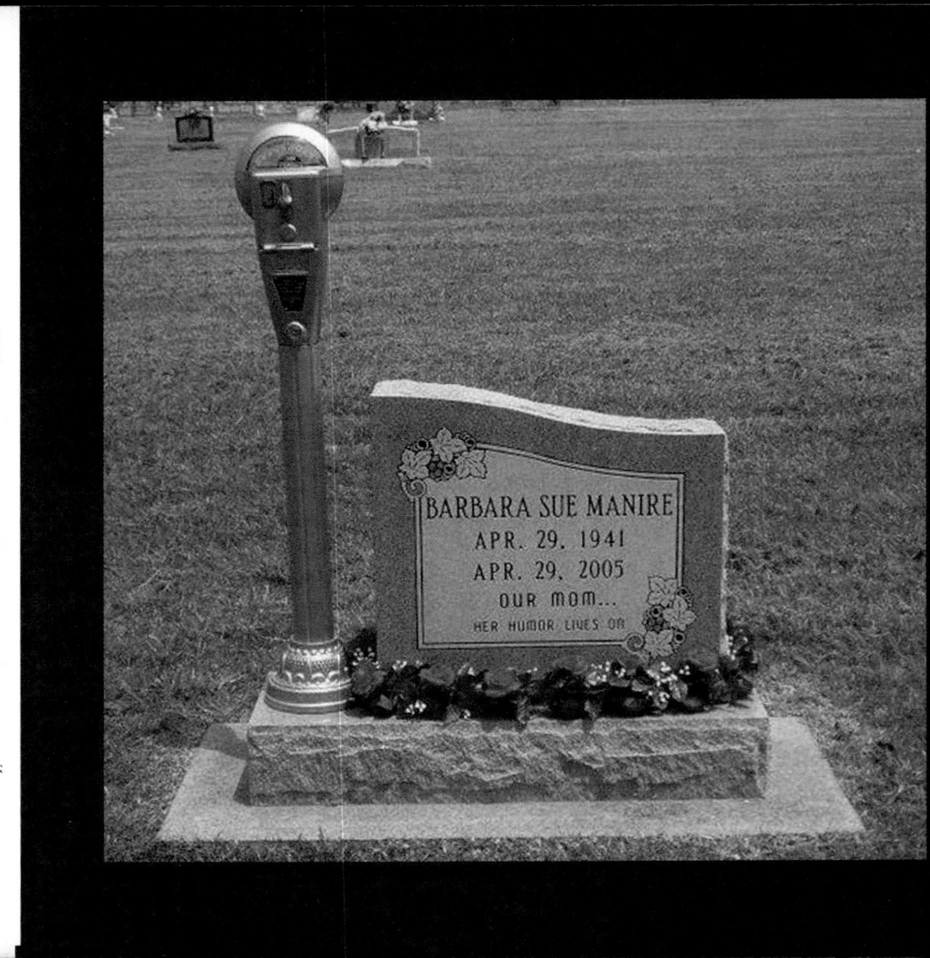

BARBARA SUE MANIRE
APR. 29. 1941
APR. 29. 2005
OUR MOM...
HER HUMOR LIVES ON

If only

we'd remembered
to feed the meter ...

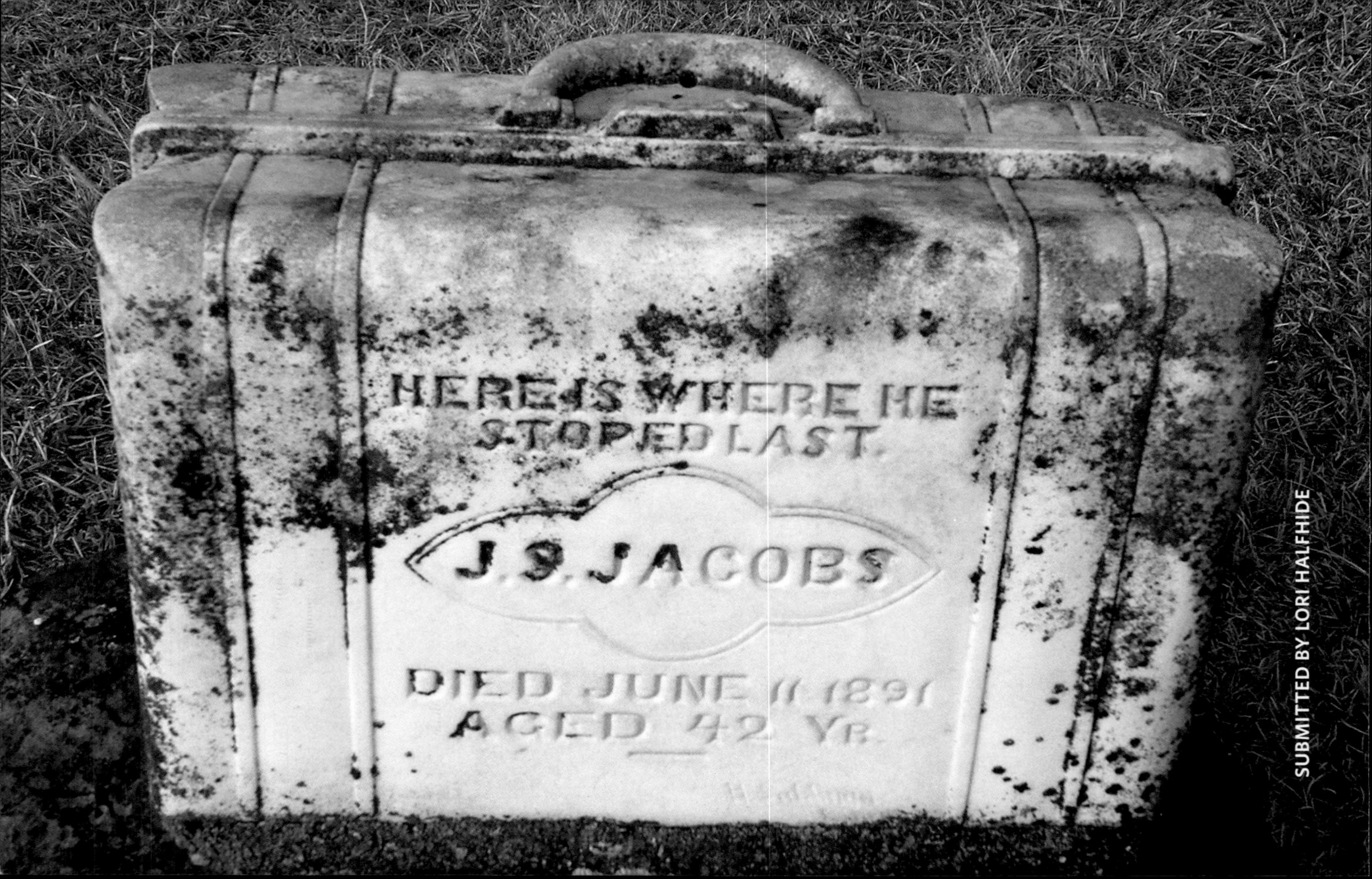
HERE IS WHERE HE
STOPED LAST.
J.S. JACOBS
DIED JUNE 11 1891
AGED 42 YR.

SUBMITTED BY LORI HALFHIDE

death
OF A SALESMAN

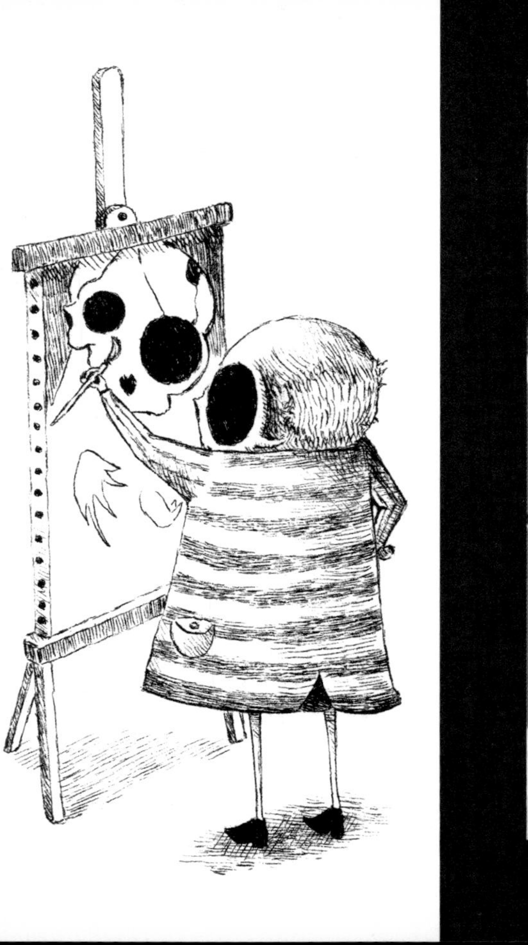

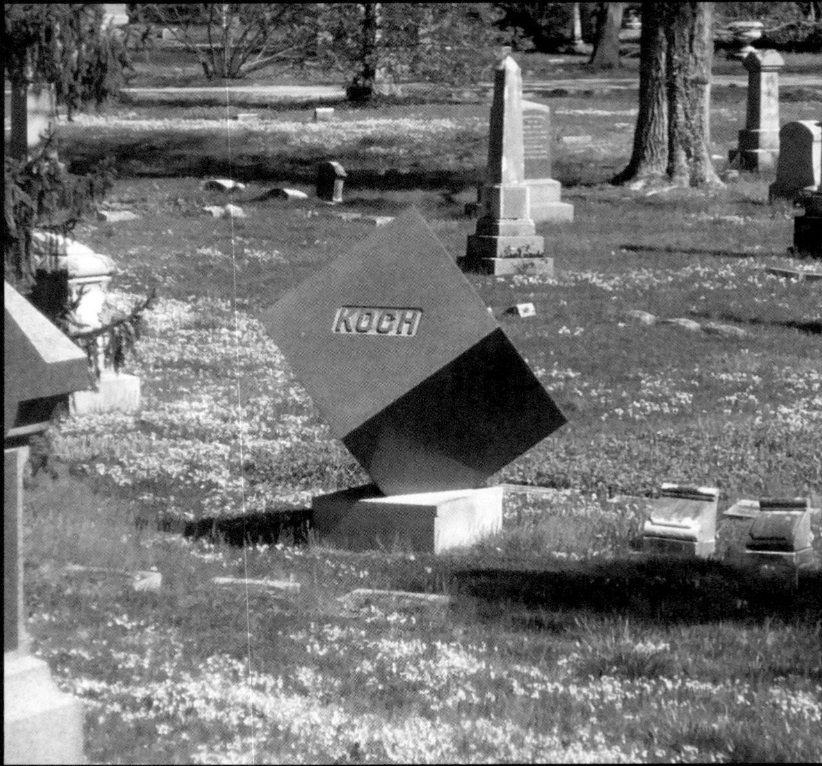
KOCH

He loved C U B I S M to death.

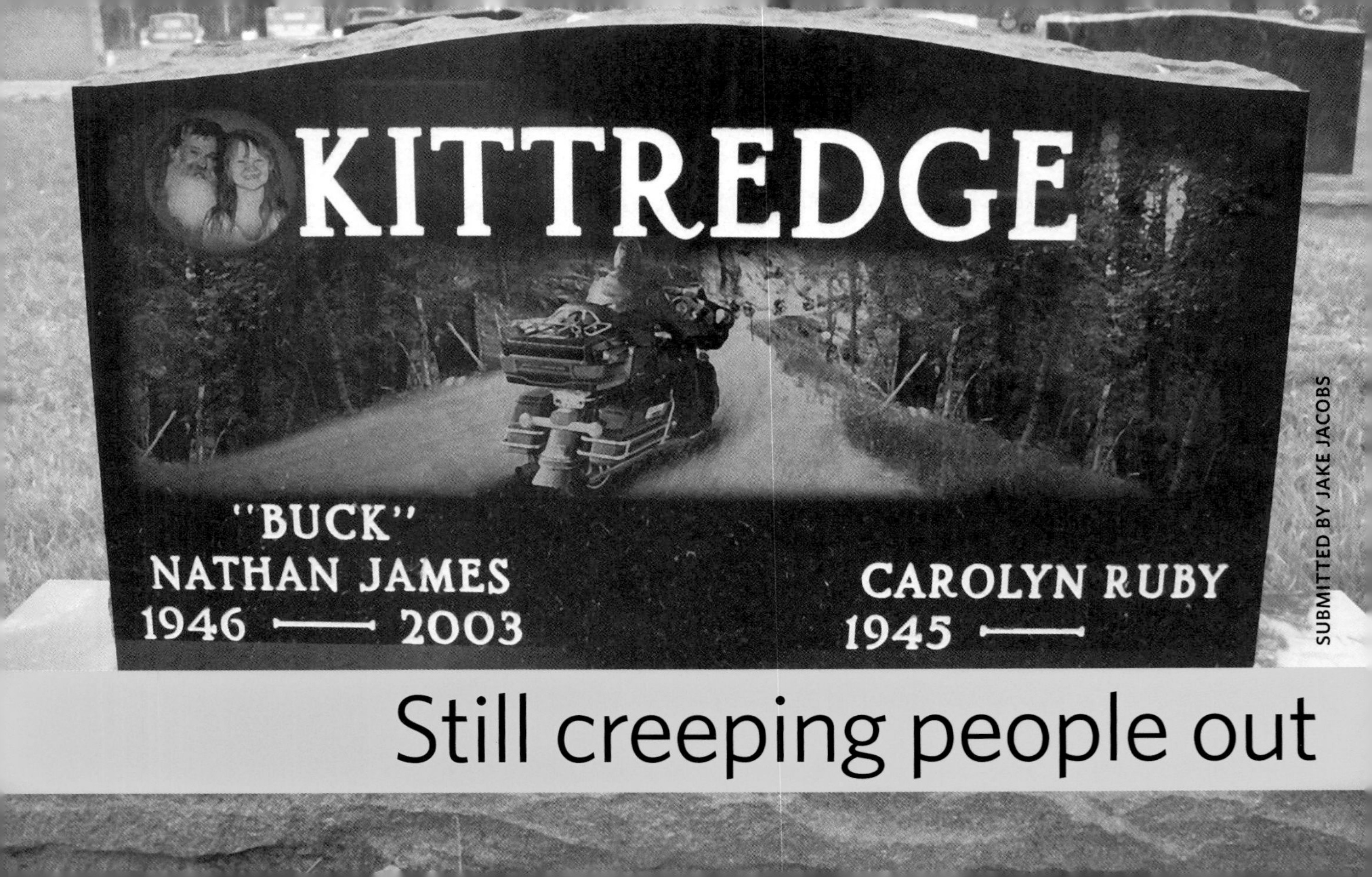
KITTREDGE
"BUCK"
NATHAN JAMES
1946 — 2003
CAROLYN RUBY
1945 —

Still creeping people out

SUBMITTED BY JAKE JACOBS

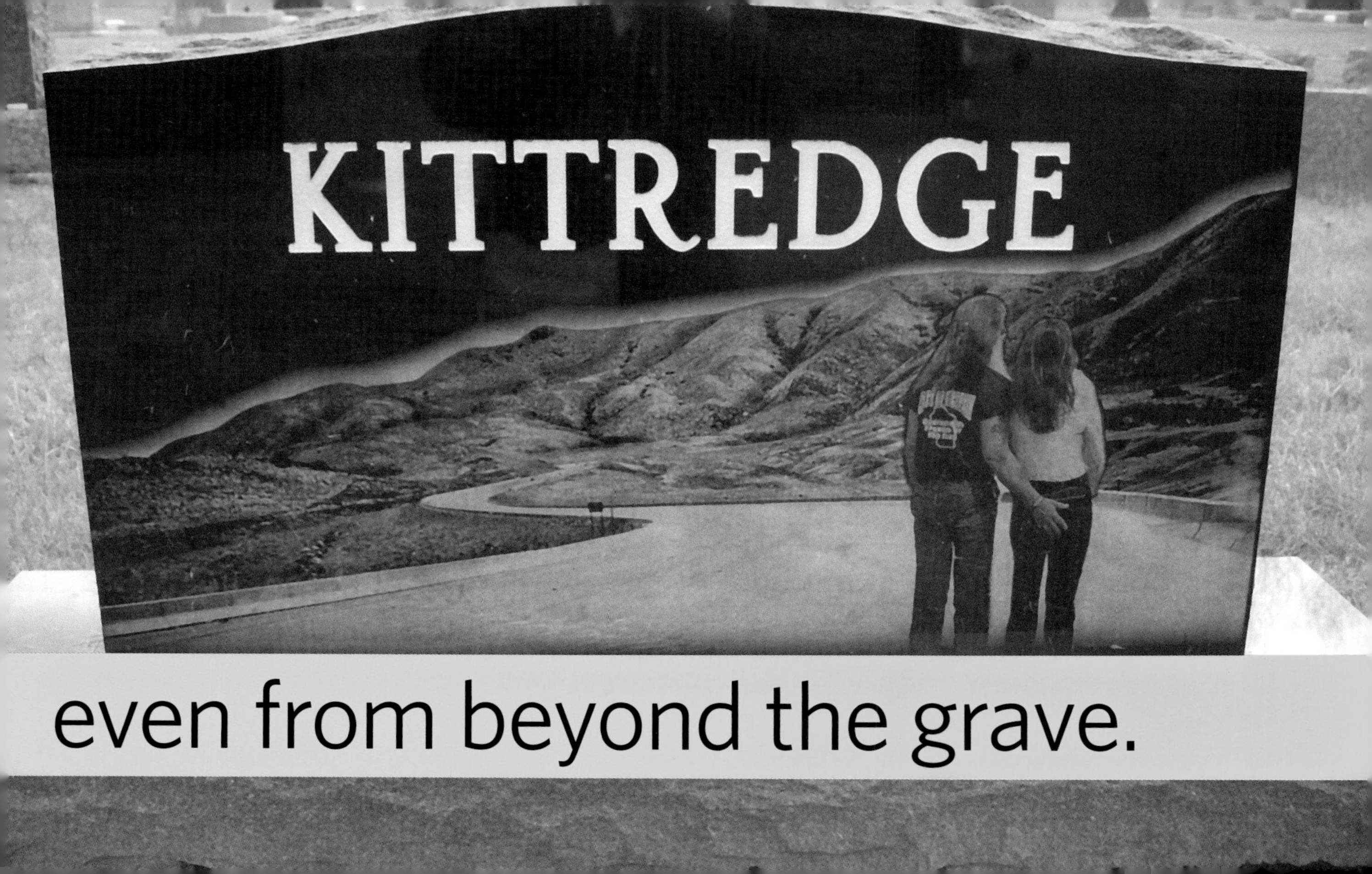
KITTREDGE

even from beyond the grave.

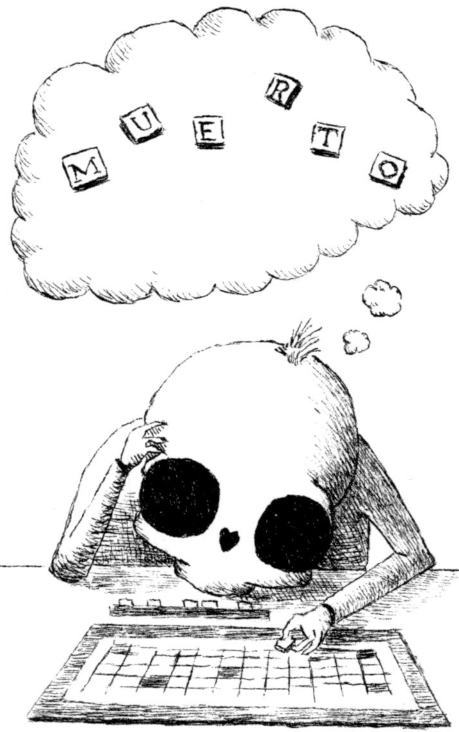
MUERTO

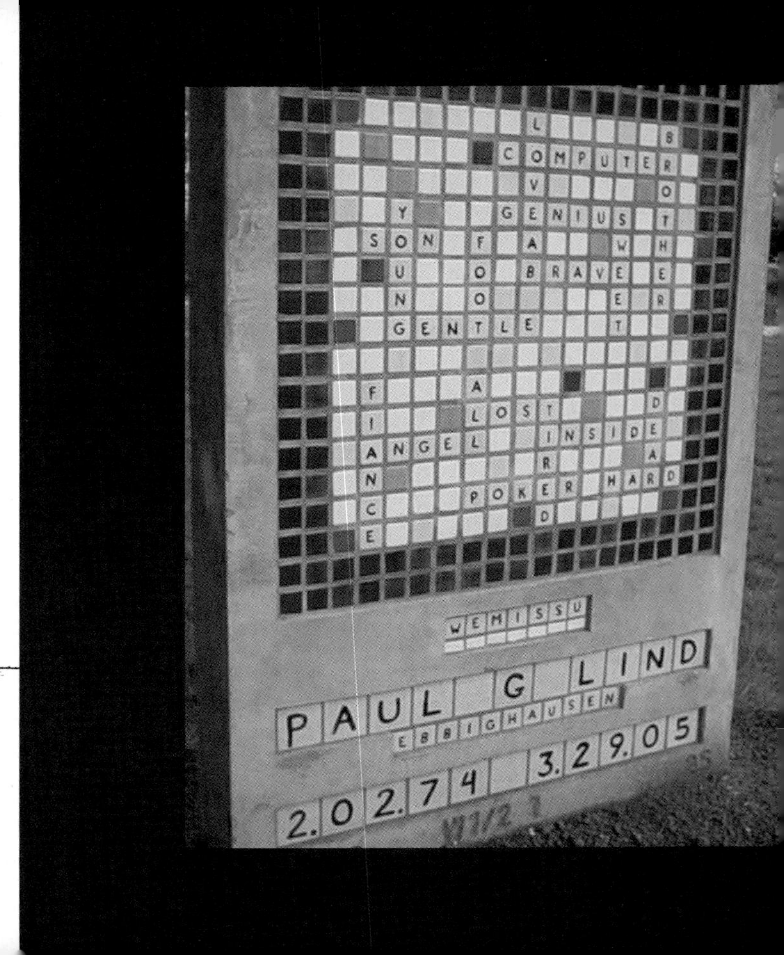
COMPUTER
GENIUS
SON
BRAVE
GENTLE
BROTHER
YOUNG
FIANCE
ANGEL
LOST
INSIDE
POKER
HARD
WEMISSU
PAUL G LIND
EBBIGHAUSEN
2.02.74 3.29.05

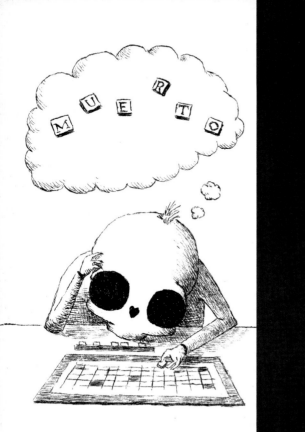

He's gone after that **triple-word score** in the **sky**

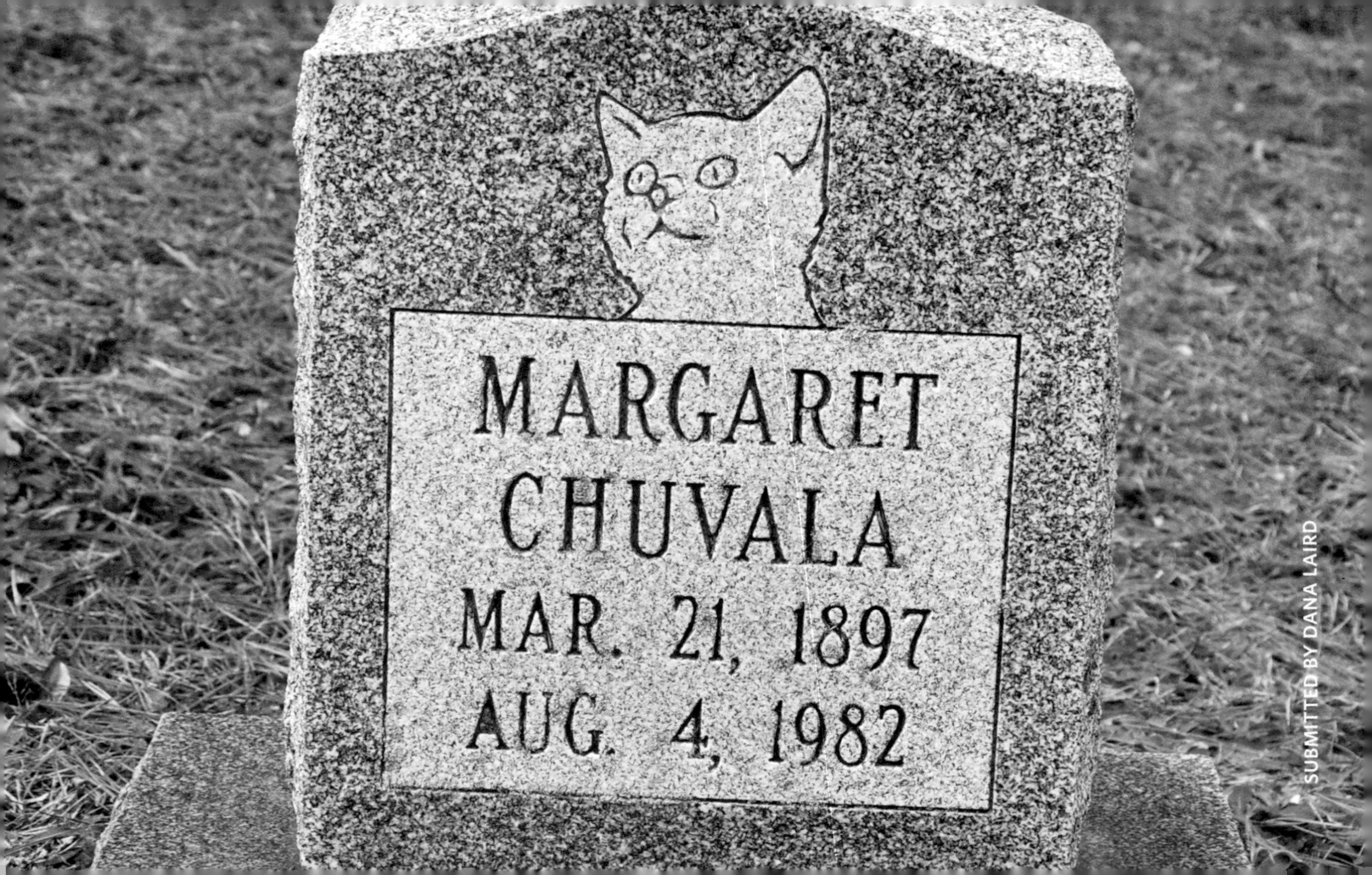
MARGARET
CHUVALA
MAR. 21, 1897
AUG. 4, 1982

SUBMITTED BY DANA LAIRD

Yes, she's dead but HERE'S A kitten!

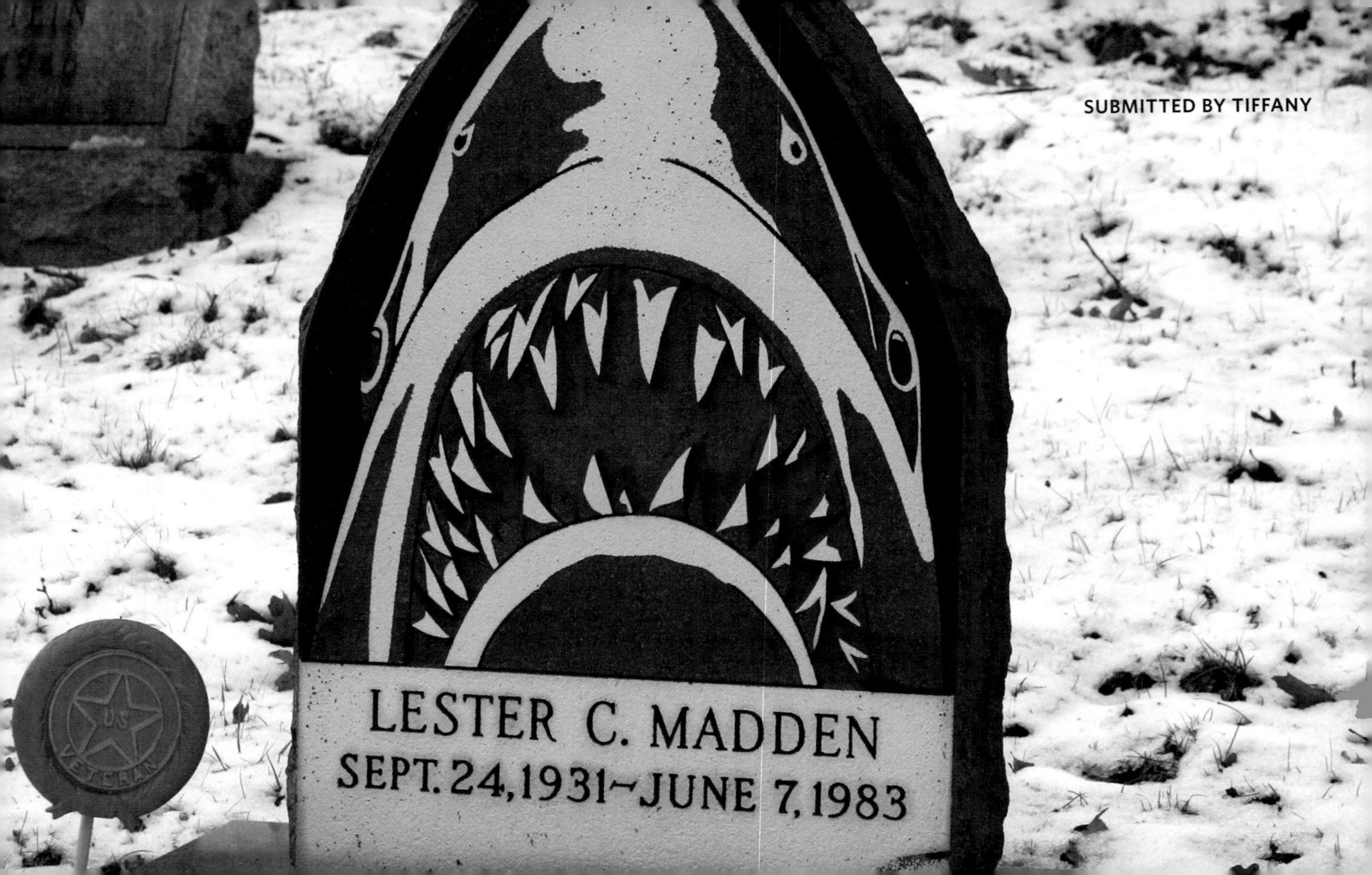
LESTER C. MADDEN
SEPT. 24, 1931~JUNE 7, 1983
U.S.
VETERAN

SUBMITTED BY TIFFANY

Cause of death: tooth infection

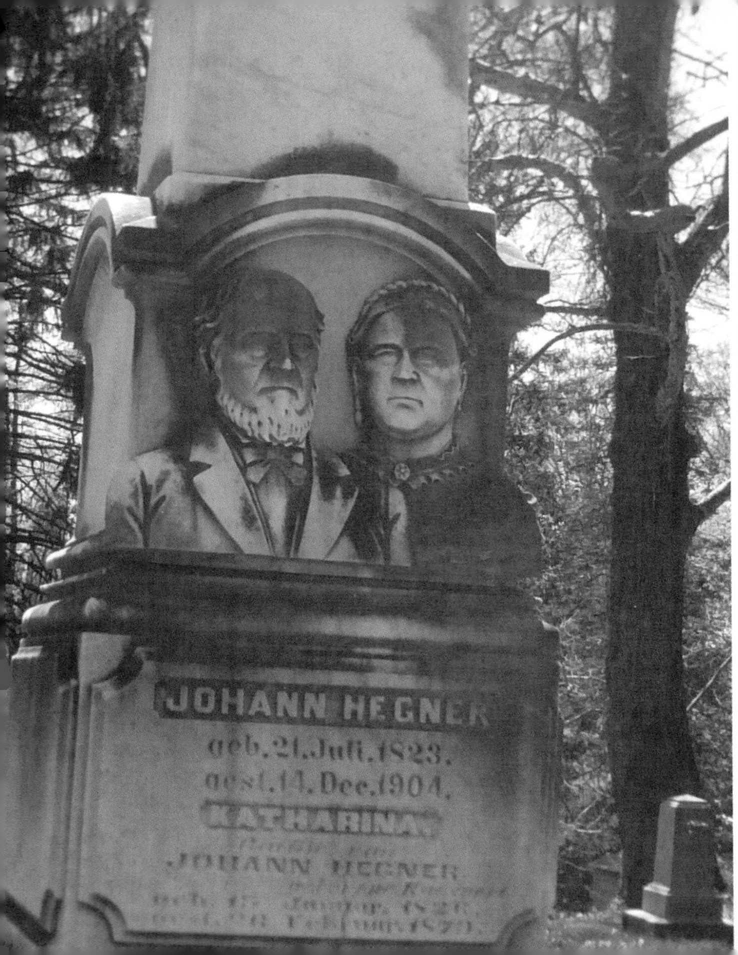
JOHANN HEGNER
geb. 21. Juli 1823.
gest. 14. Dec. 1904.
KATHARINA
JOHANN HEGNER

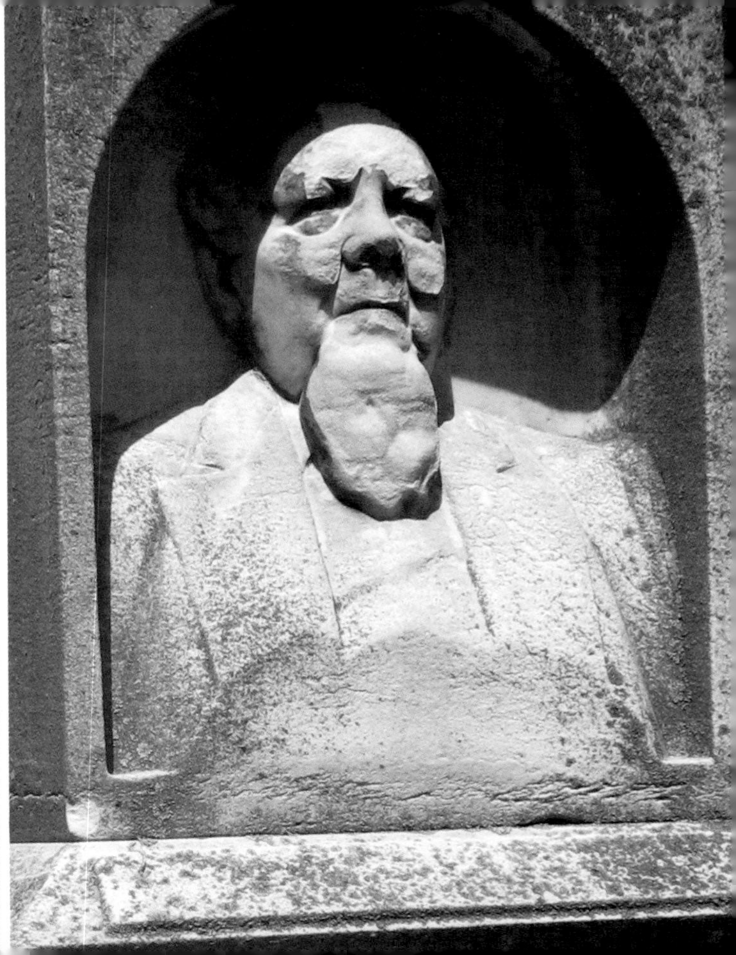

So their children will **NEVER** forget their **loving** faces

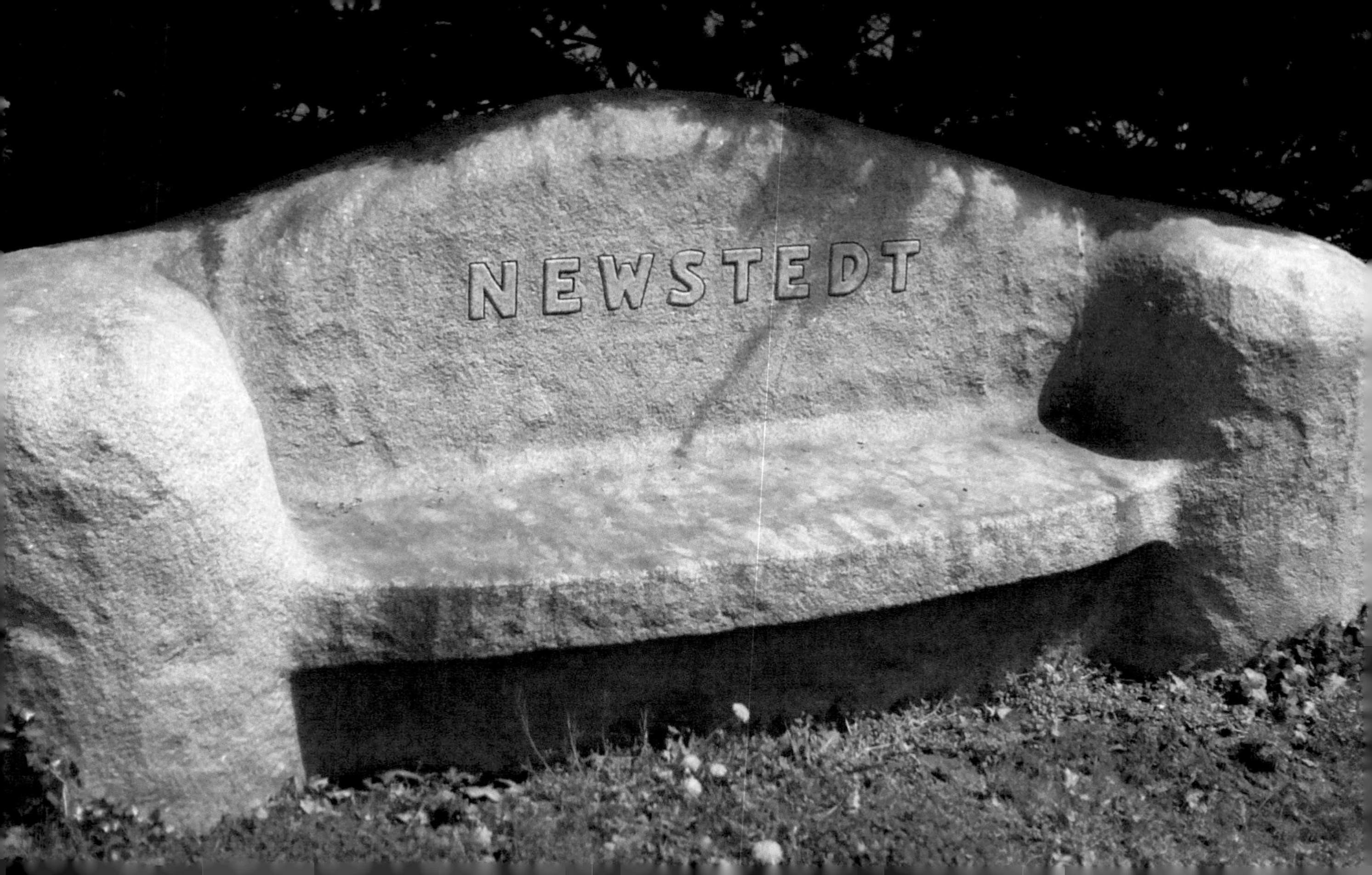
NEWSTEDT

Loaf in Peace

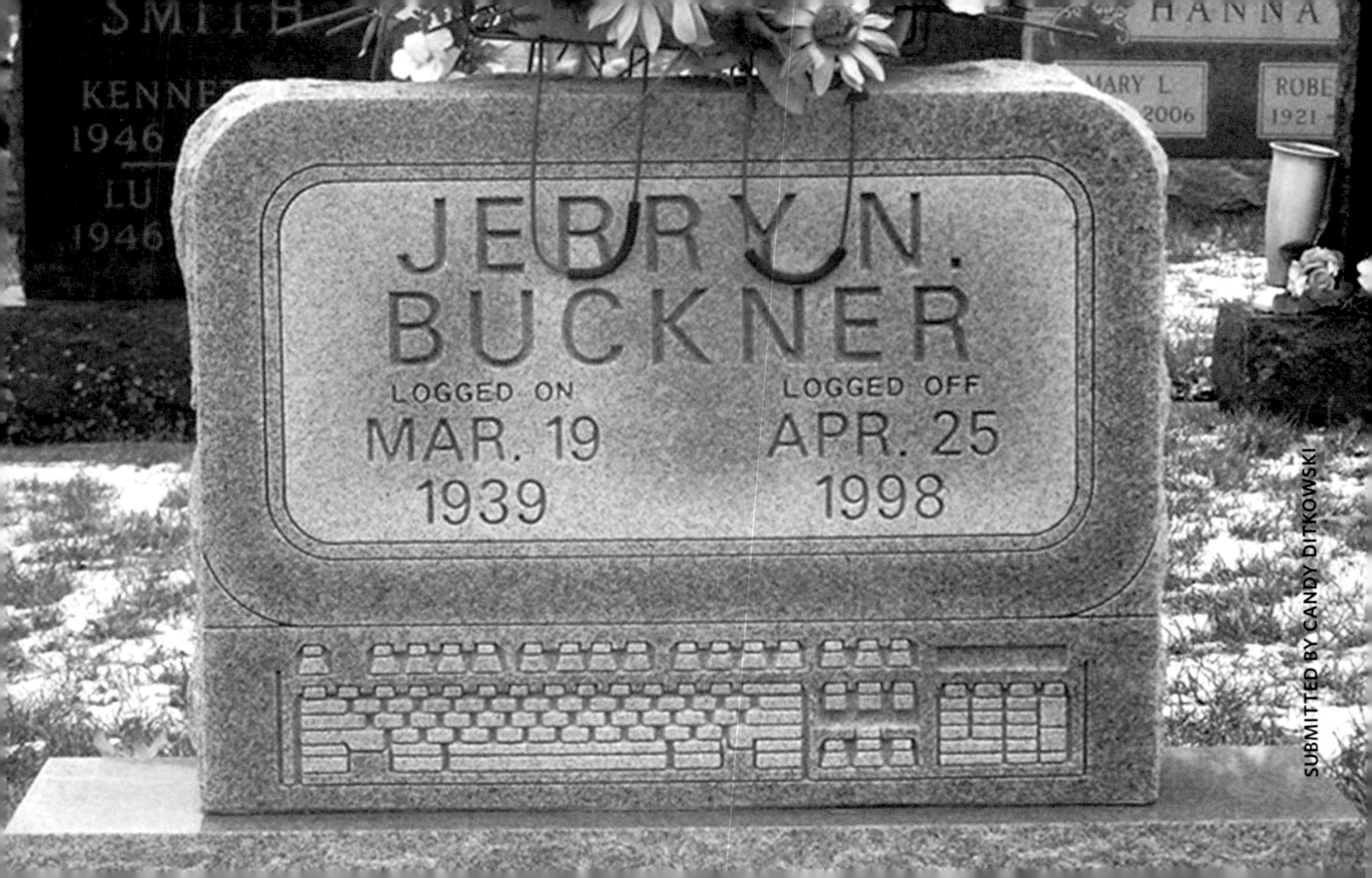
JERRY N.
BUCKNER
LOGGED ON
MAR. 19
1939
LOGGED OFF
APR. 25
1998

SUBMITTED BY CANDY DITKOWSKI

If only
the IT guys had gotten there
sooner....

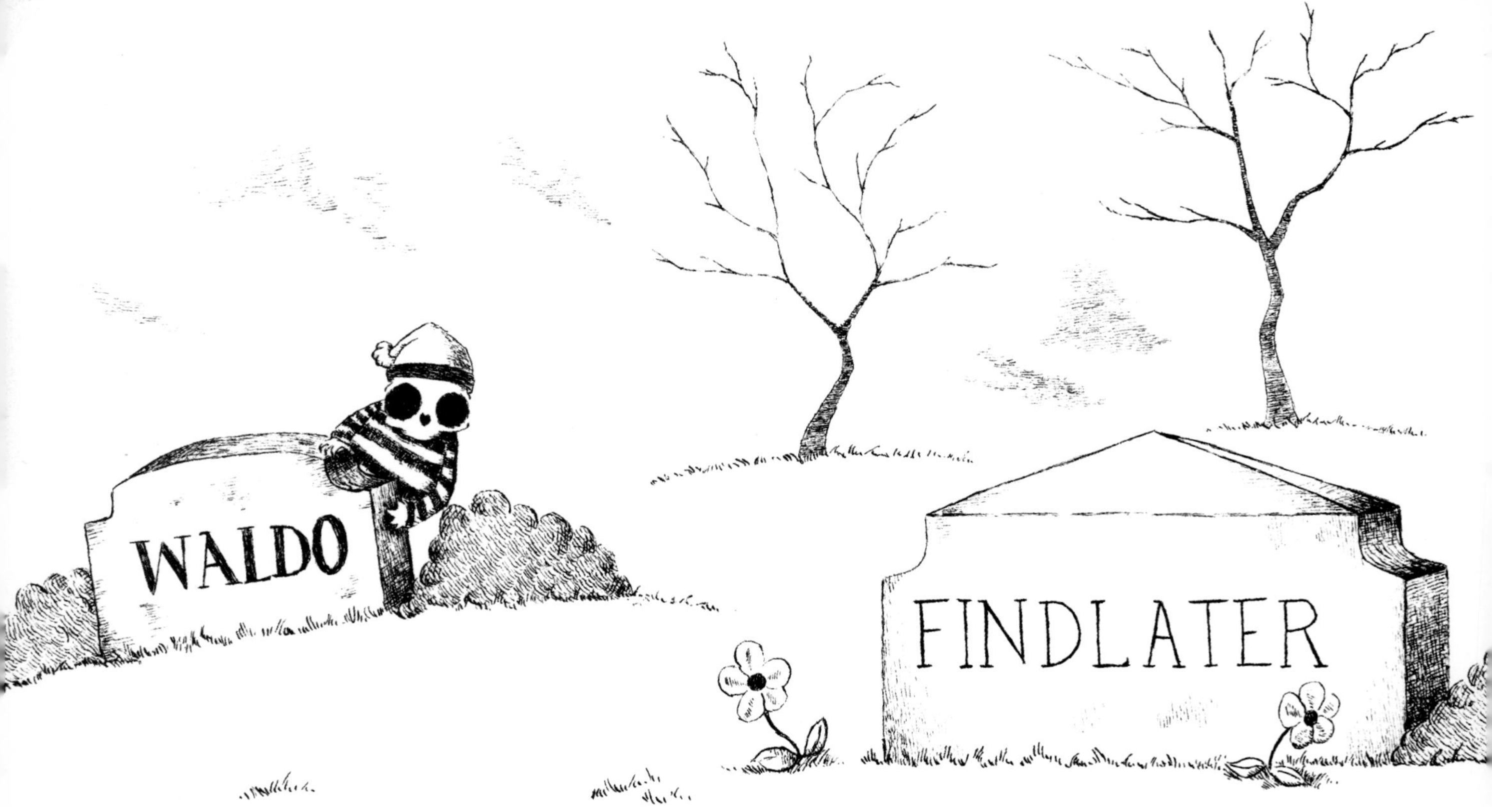
WALDO
FINDLATER

DUMM
AND DUMMER

Rib-tickling eternal pairings

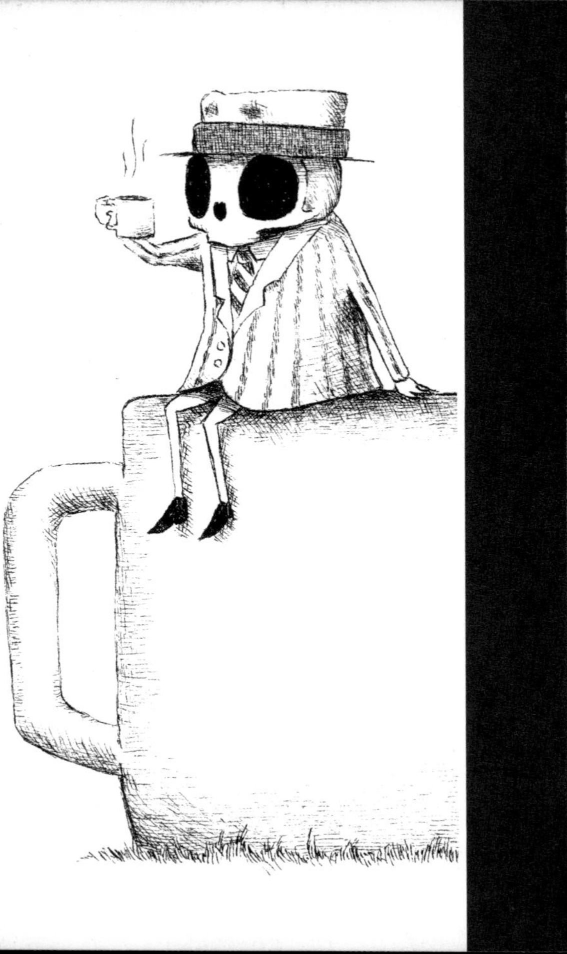

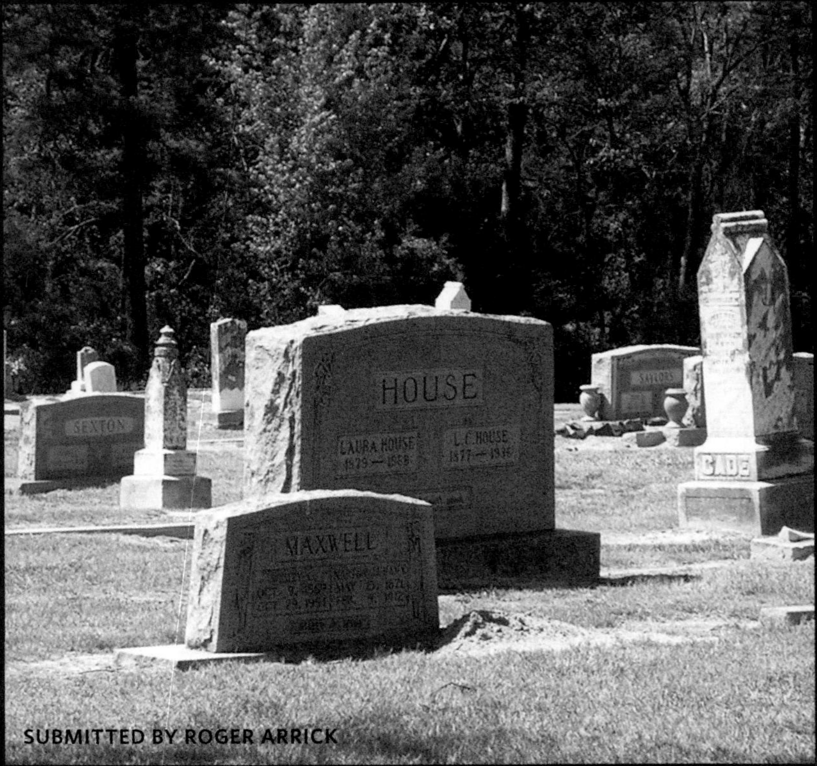
HOUSE
LAURA HOUSE
L.C. HOUSE
SEXTON
MAXWELL
CADE
SUBMITTED BY ROGER ARRICK

Dead to the last drop.

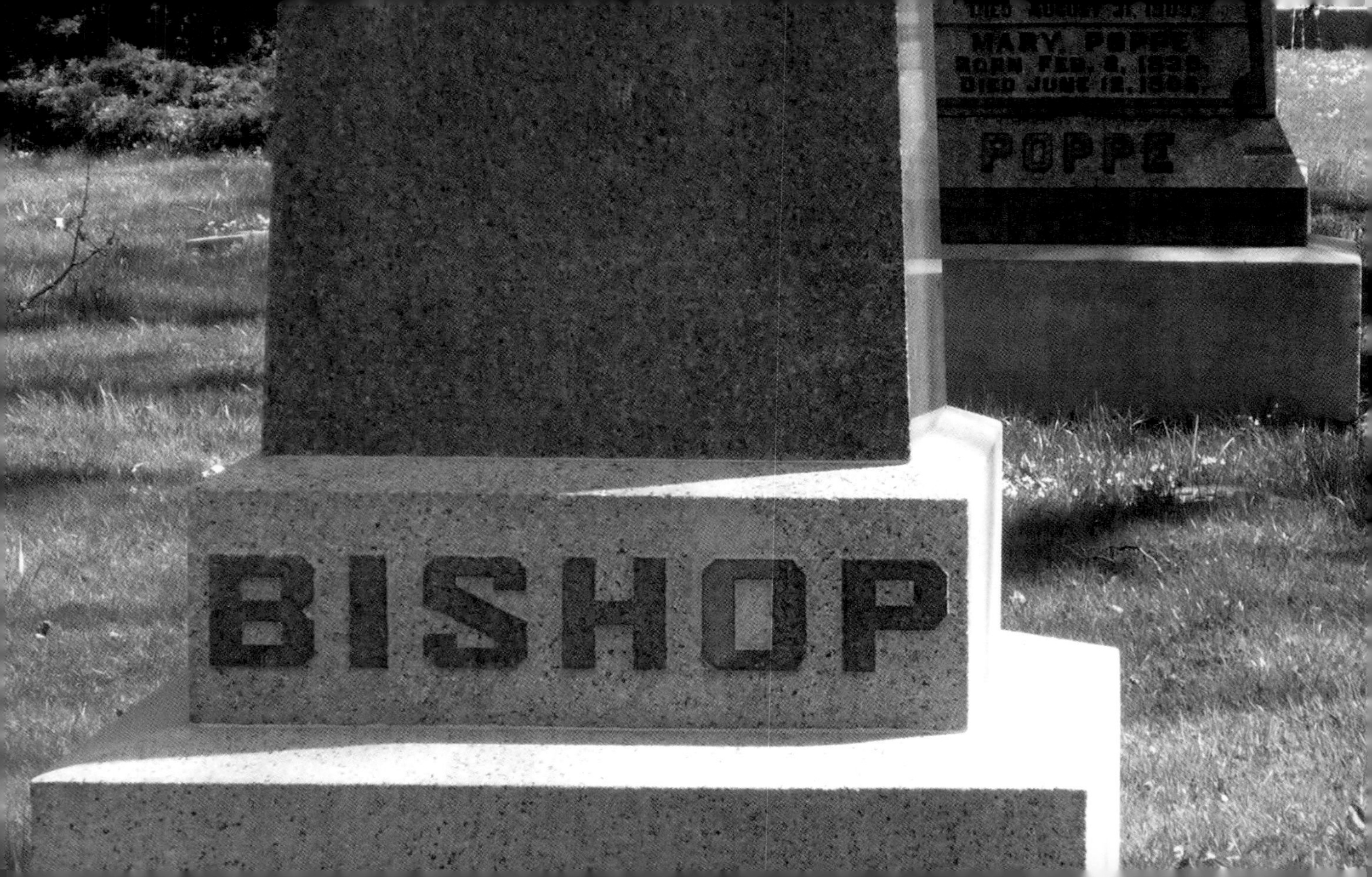
MARY POPPE
POPPE
BISHOP

STONECUTTER'S CONFESSION:
Forgive me, Lord, for I have misspelled.

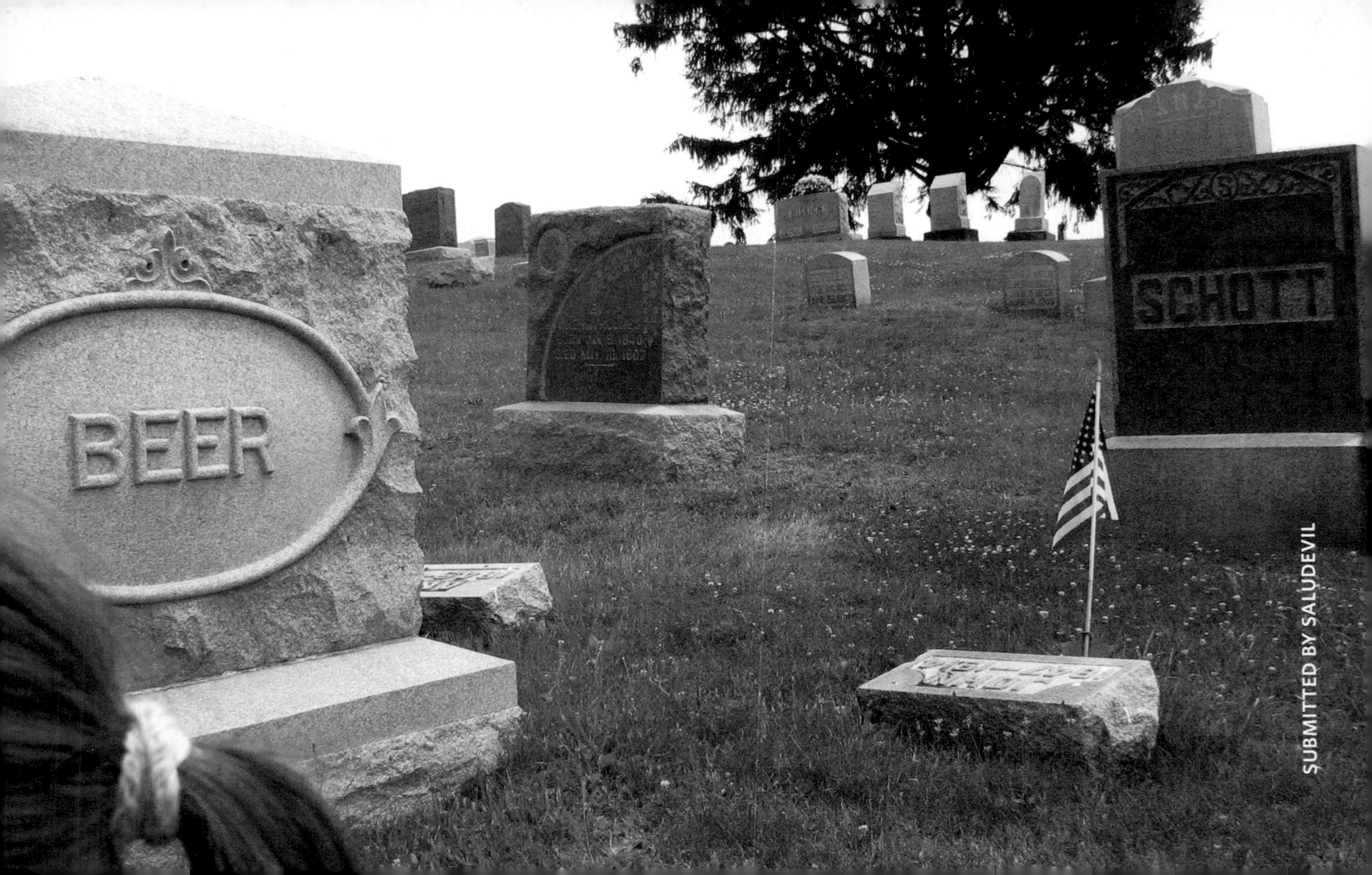
BEER
SCHOTT

SUBMITTED BY SALUDEVIL

what happened
TO BOURBON?

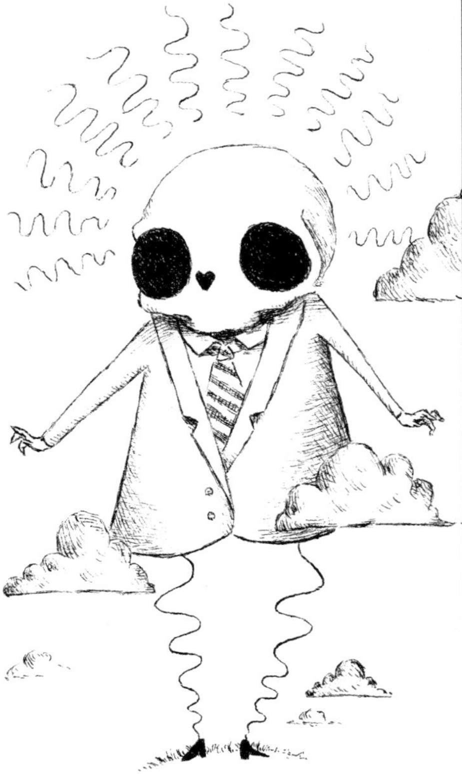

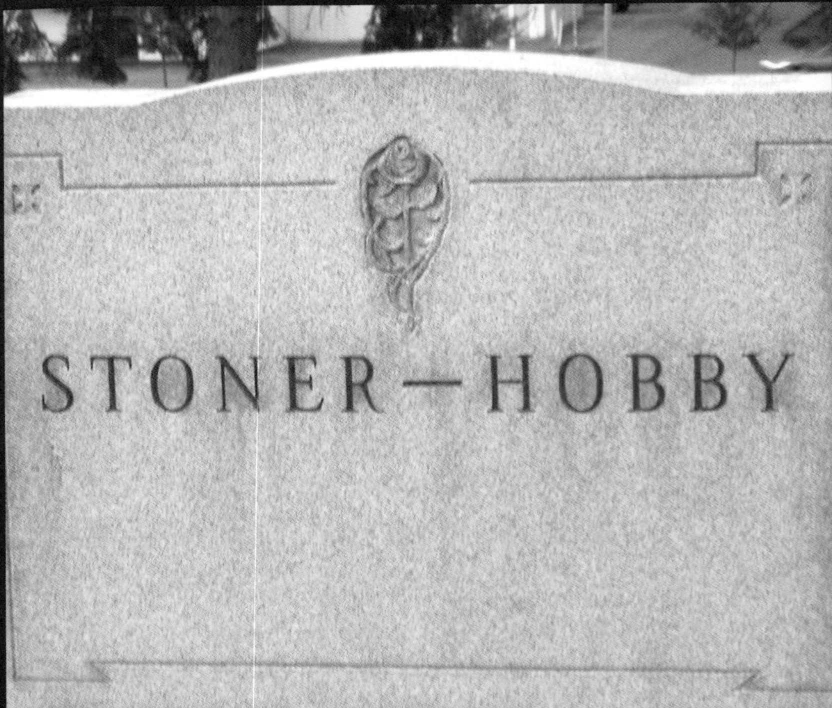
STONER—HOBBY

SUBMITTED BY NIKORETRO

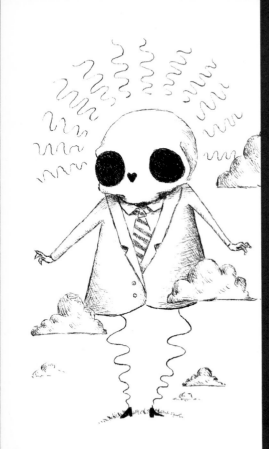

Dude!

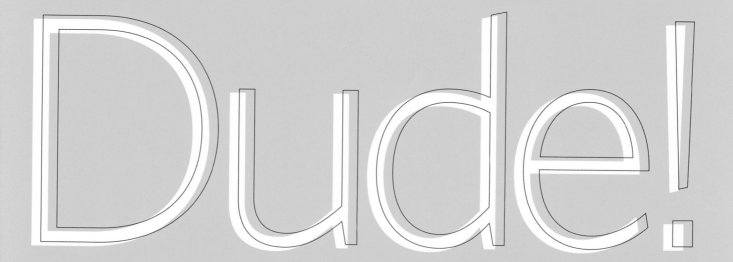

FRENCH

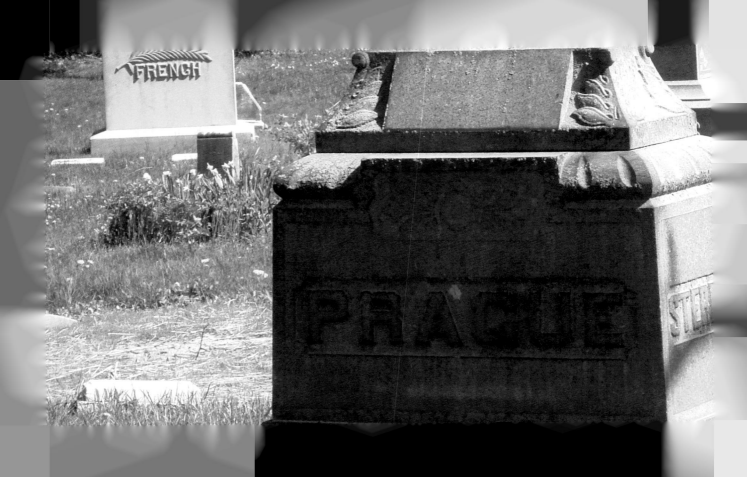

Made a wrong turn
on that European vacation, eh?

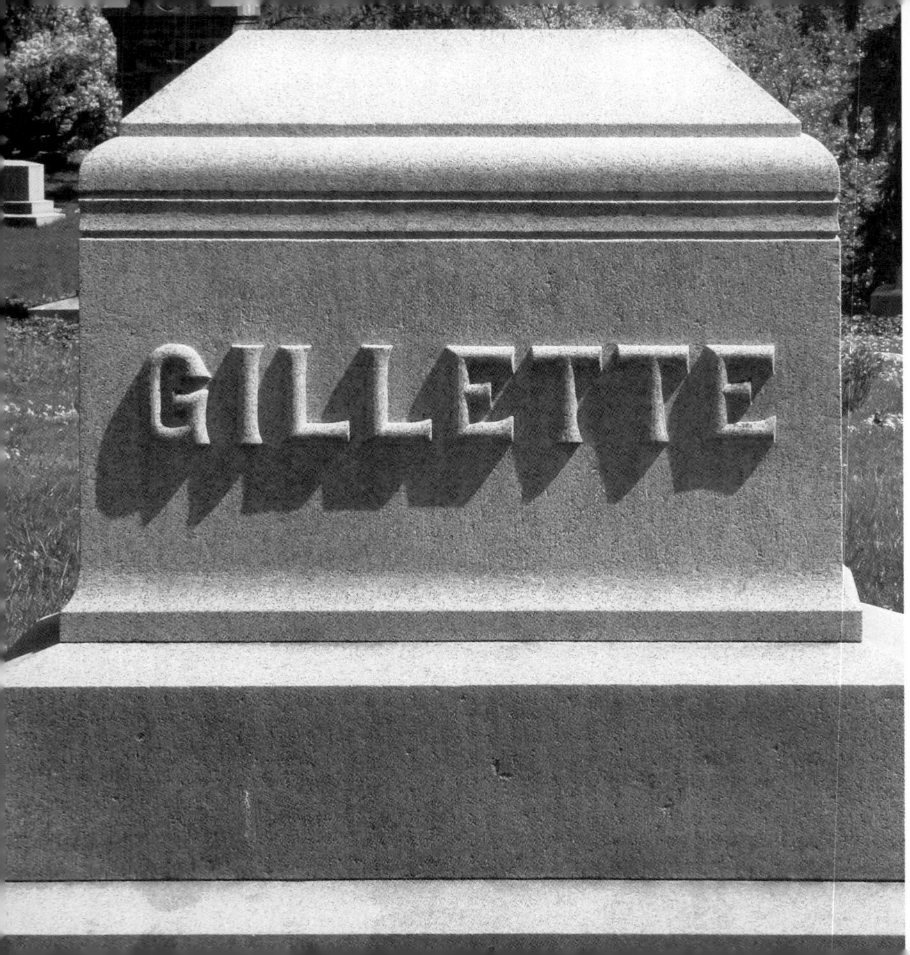
GILLETTE

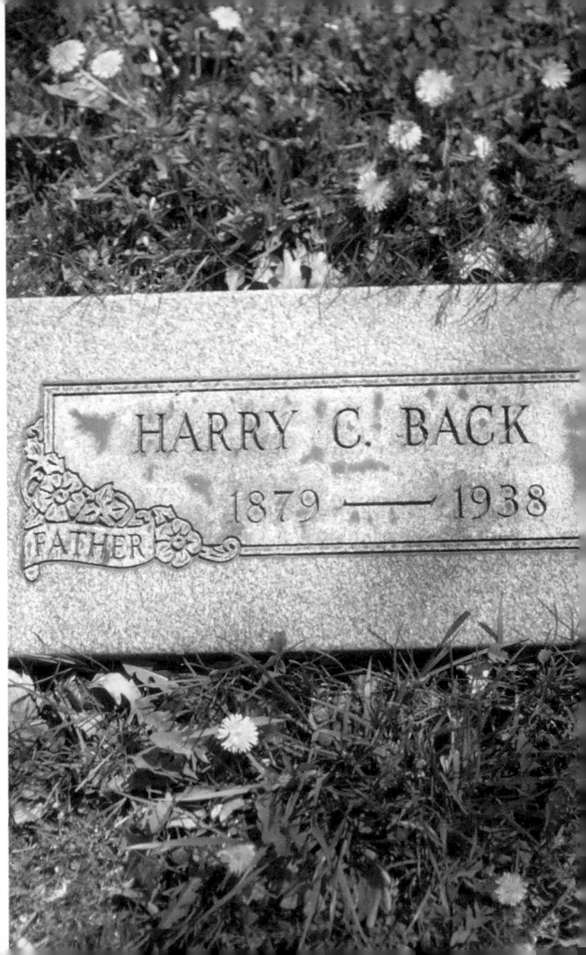
HARRY C. BACK
1879 — 1938
FATHER

A match made in
heaven. ♥

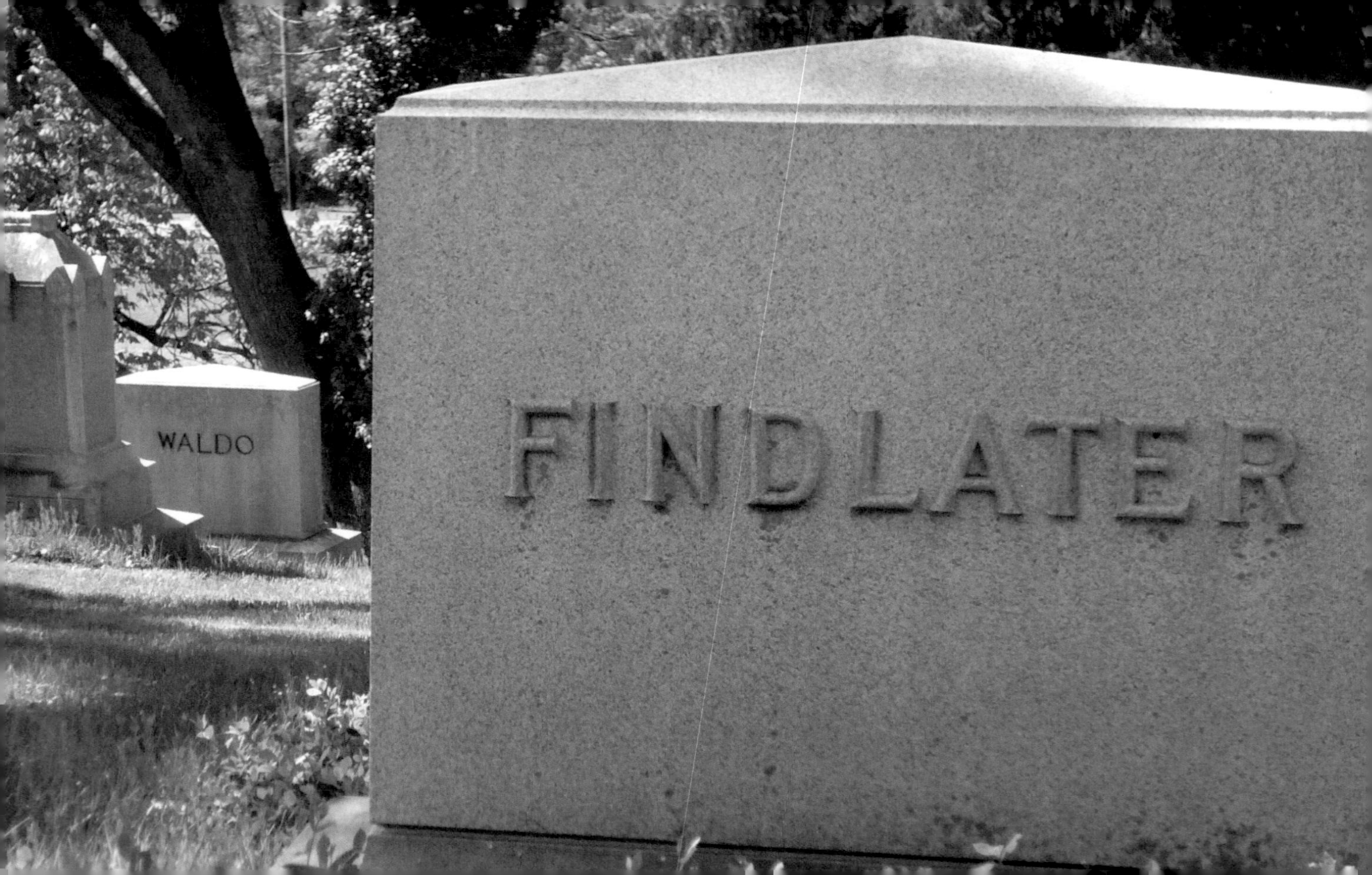
WALDO
FINDLATER

Where is he?

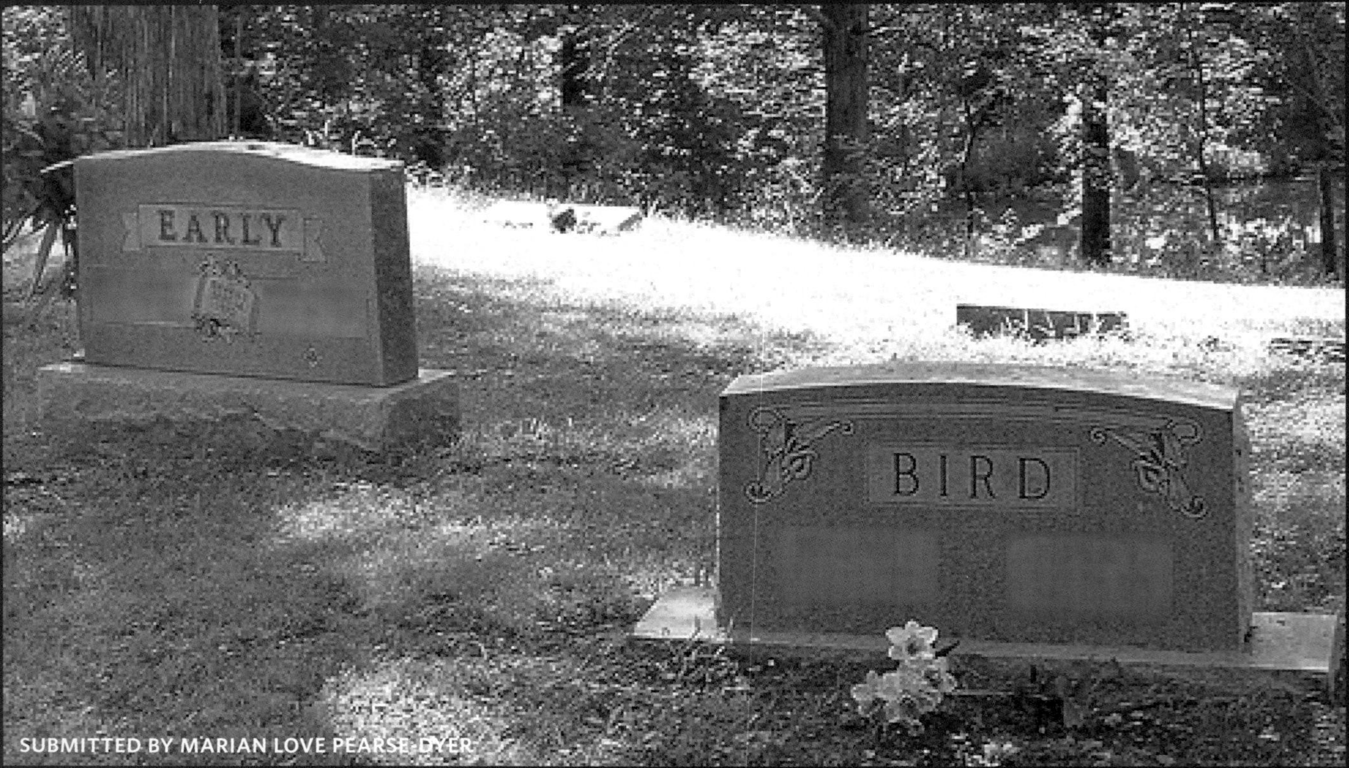
EARLY
BIRD

SUBMITTED BY MARIAN LOVE PEARSE-DYER

The early bird gets the good cemetery plot.

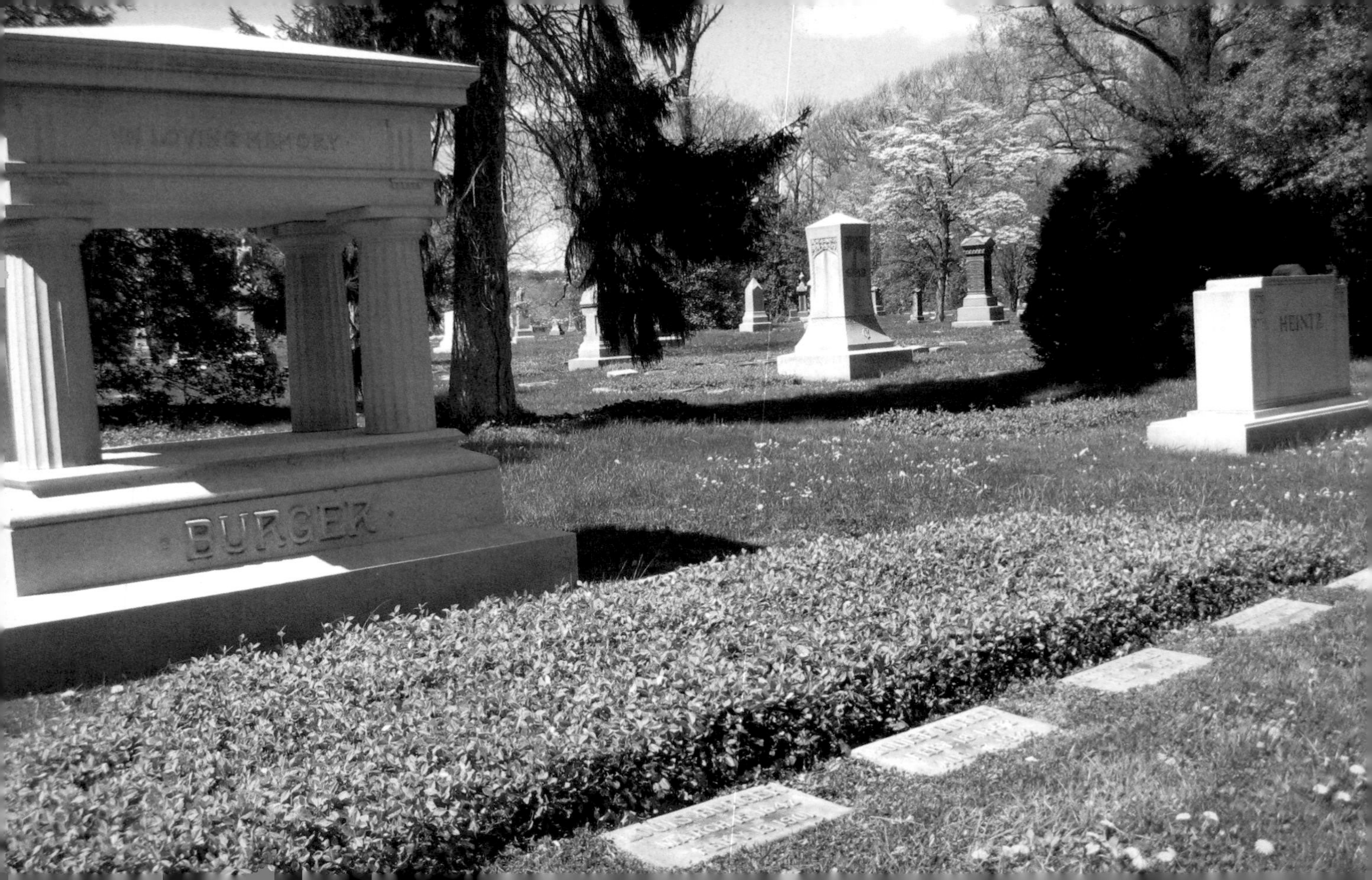
BURGER
HEINTZ

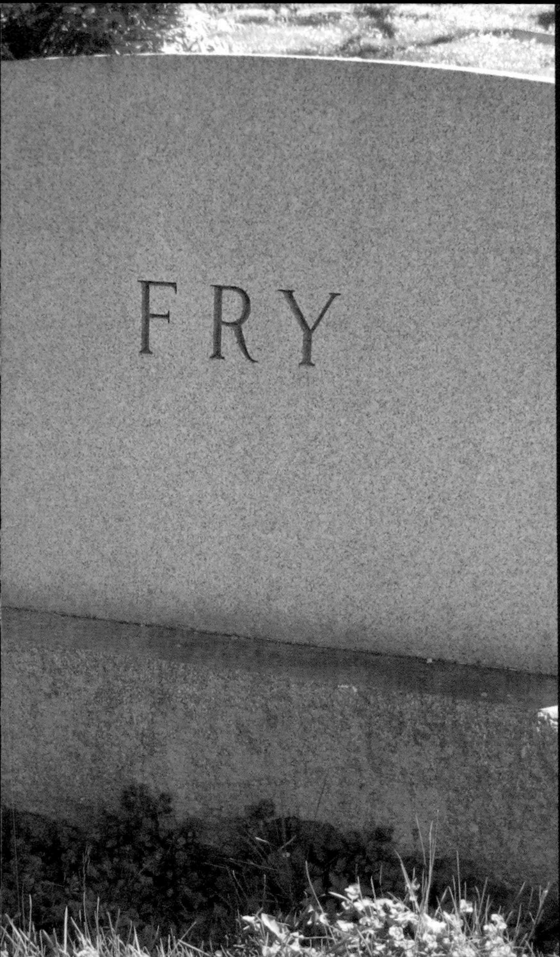
FRY

Death has
never been
so tasty!

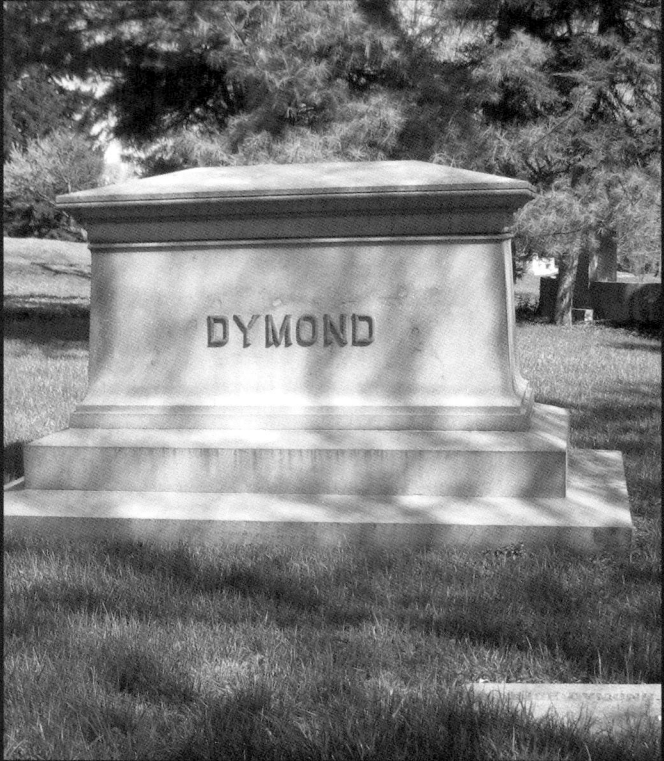
DYMOND

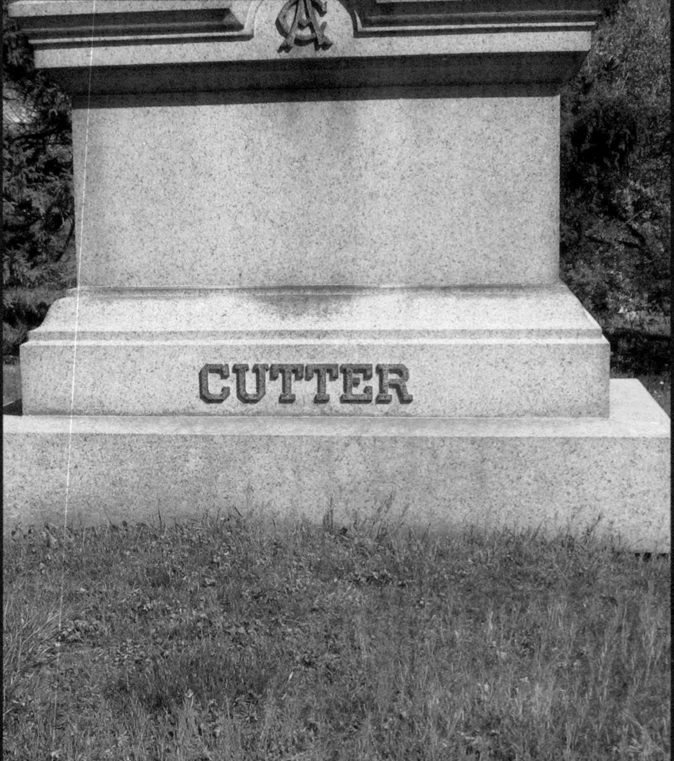
CUTTER

Buried treasure?

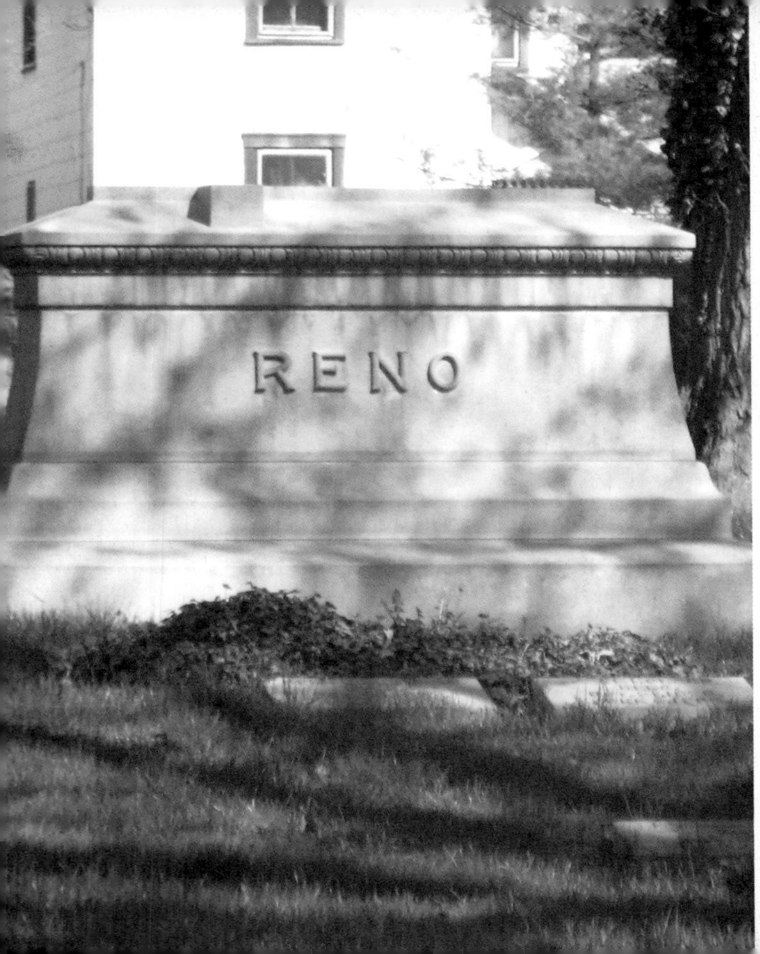
RENO

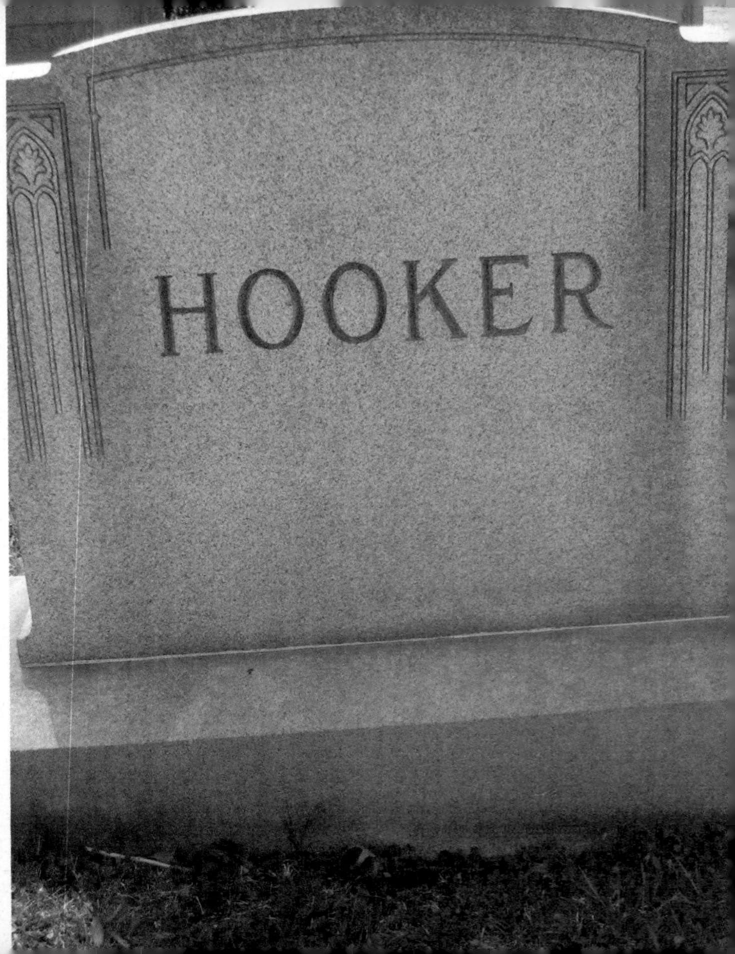
HOOKER

Call 911!

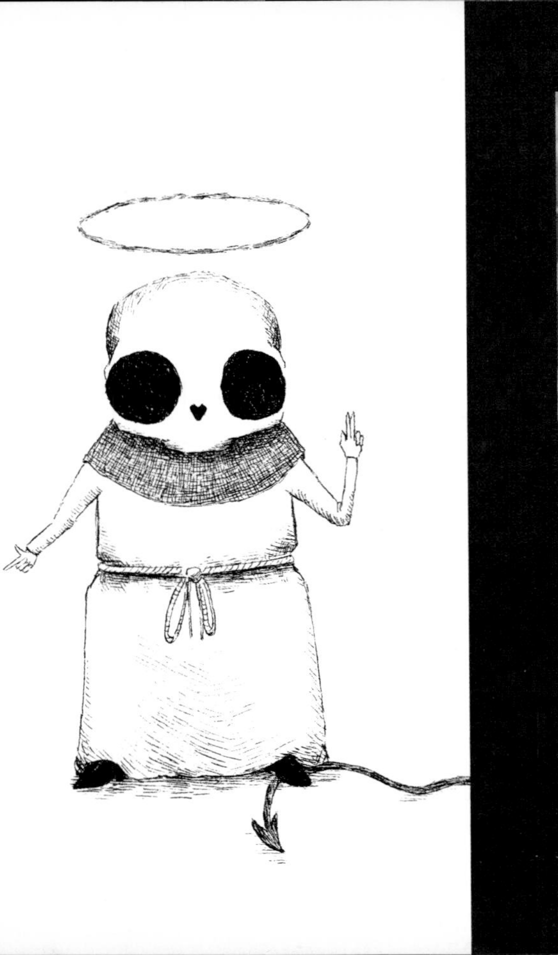

SUBMITTED BY S. PATRICK MORGAN

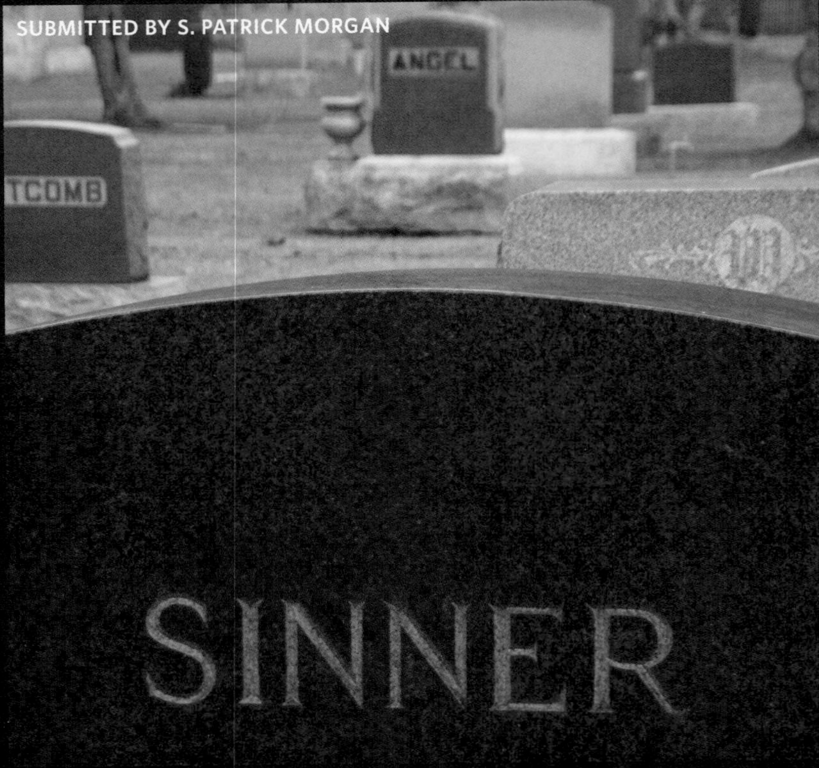
ANGEL
TCOMB
SINNER

The battle of
GOOD AND EVIL
finally put to rest

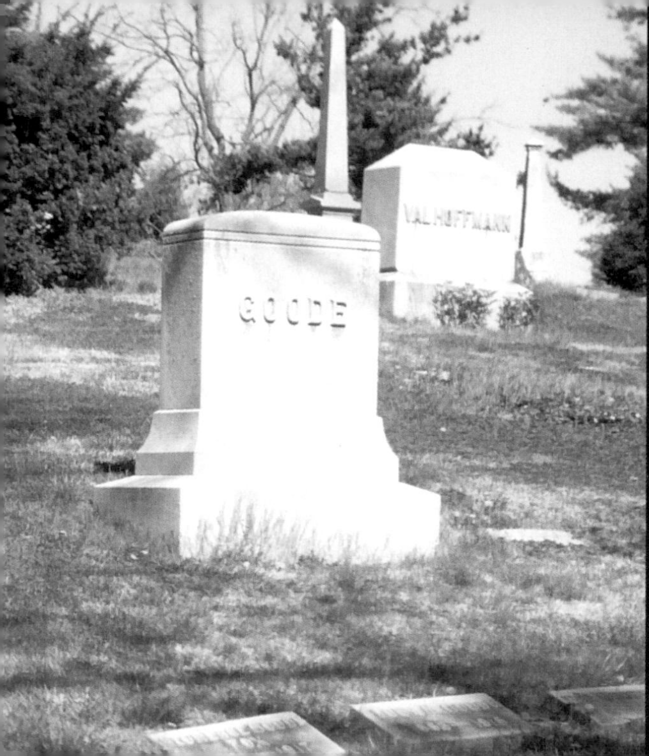
VAL HOFFMANN
GOODE

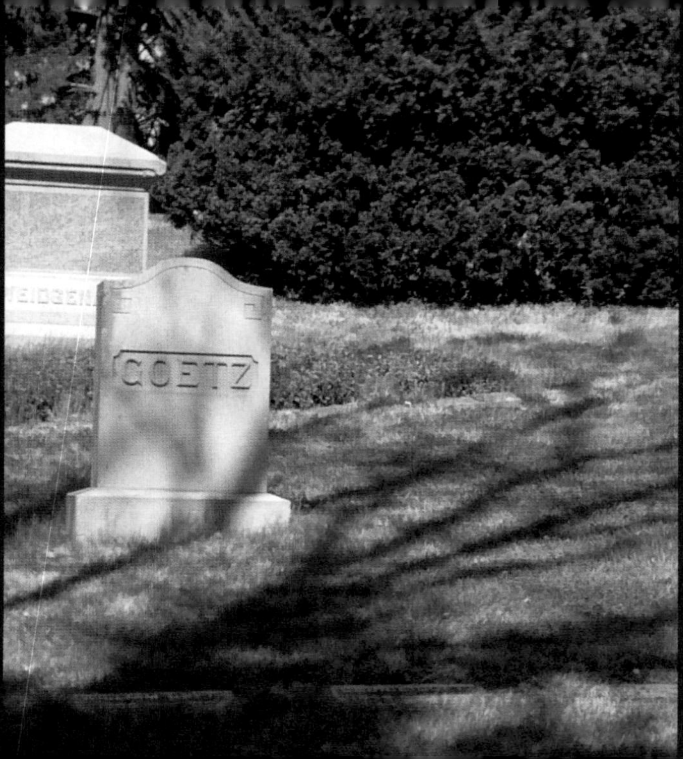
GOETZ

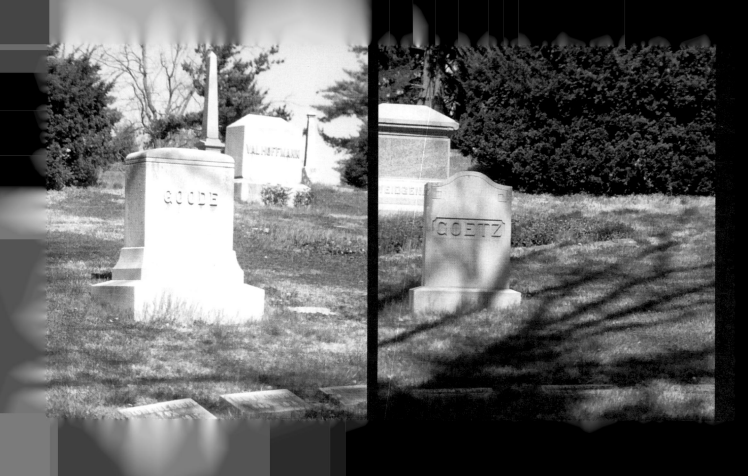

It doesn't get any better than this.

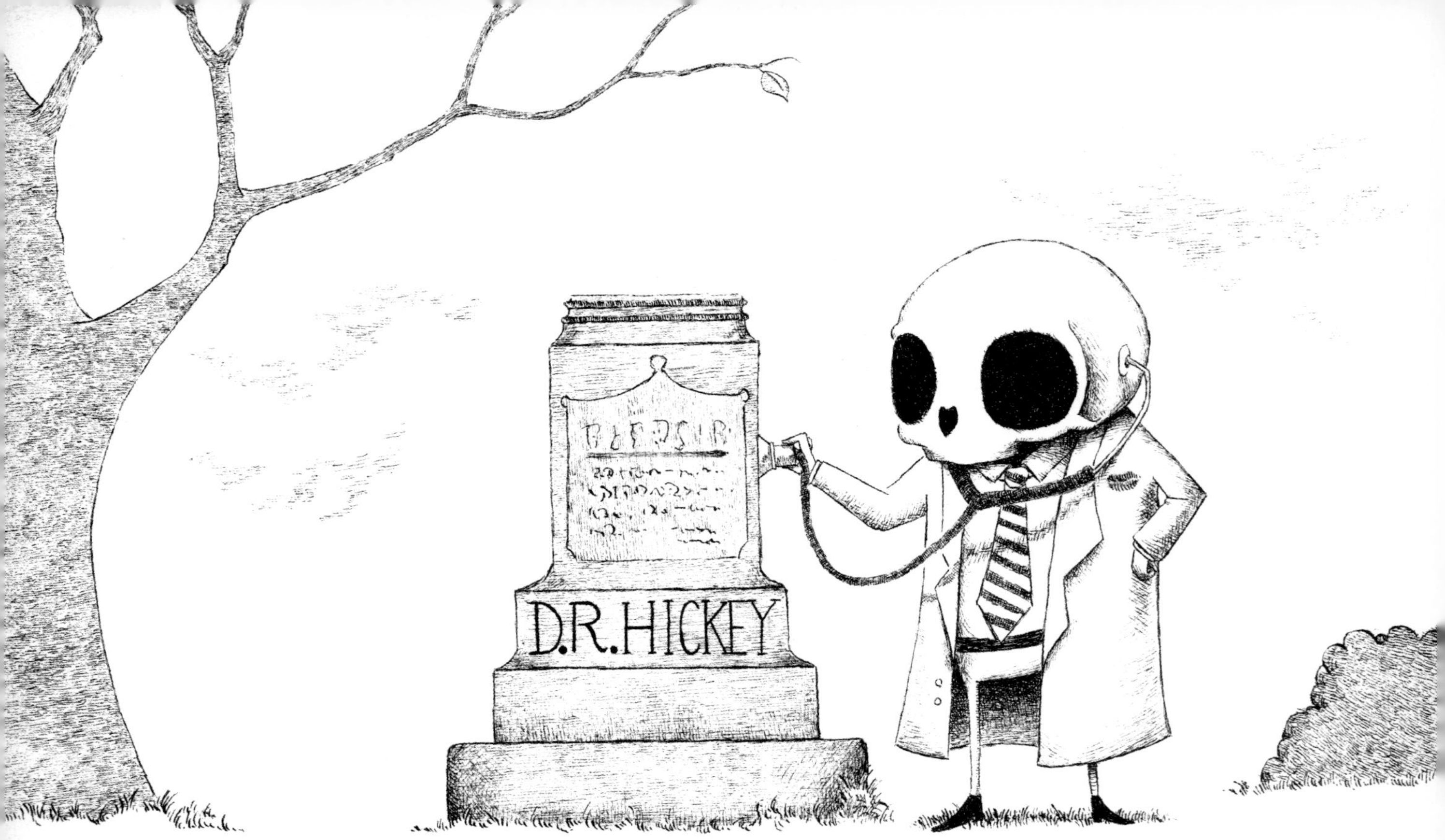
D.R.HICKEY

DIE

LAUGHING

Monuments to utterly unfortunate last names

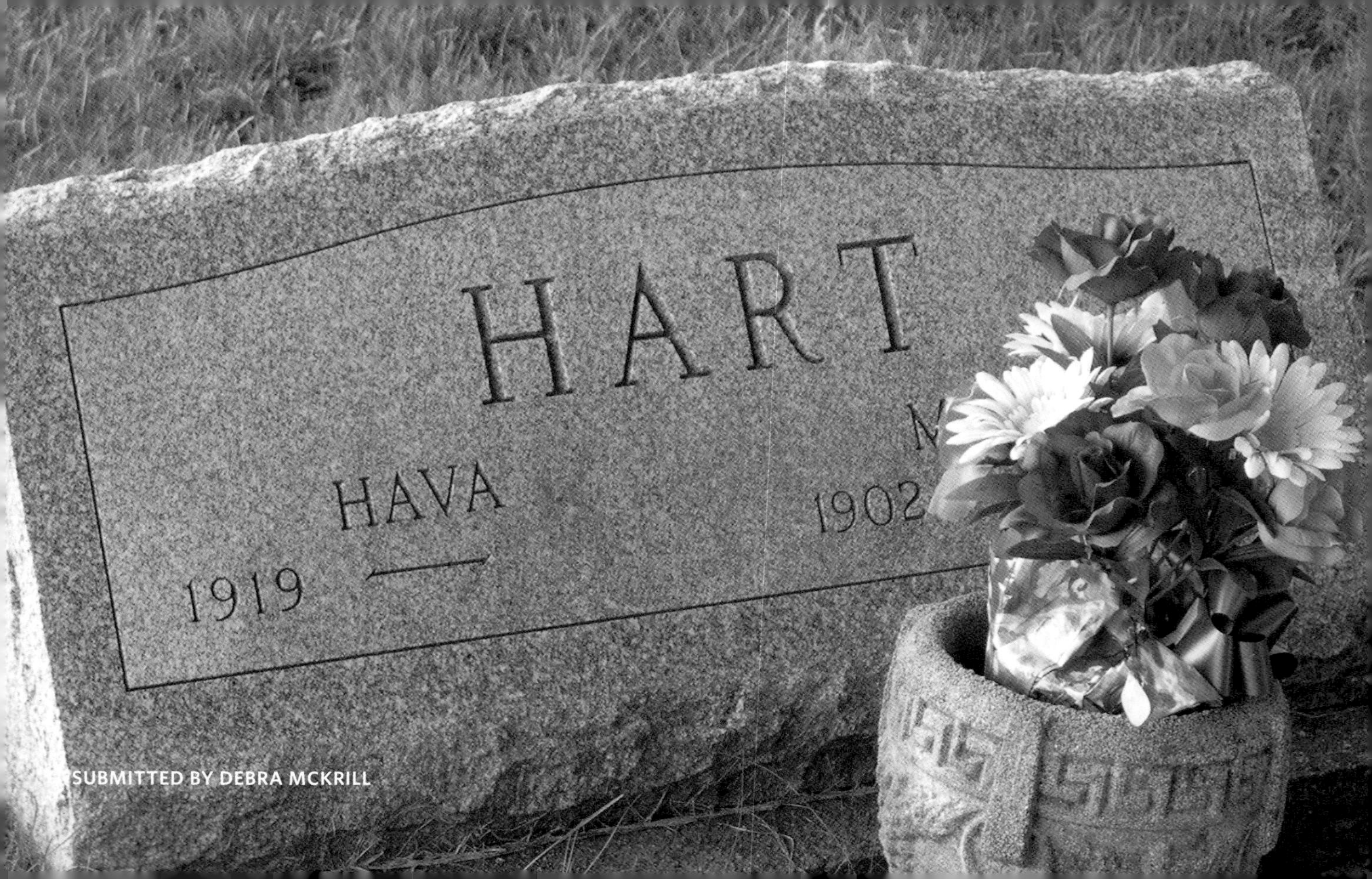
HART
HAVA
1919
M
1902

SUBMITTED BY DEBRA MCKRILL

Infamous
last
words

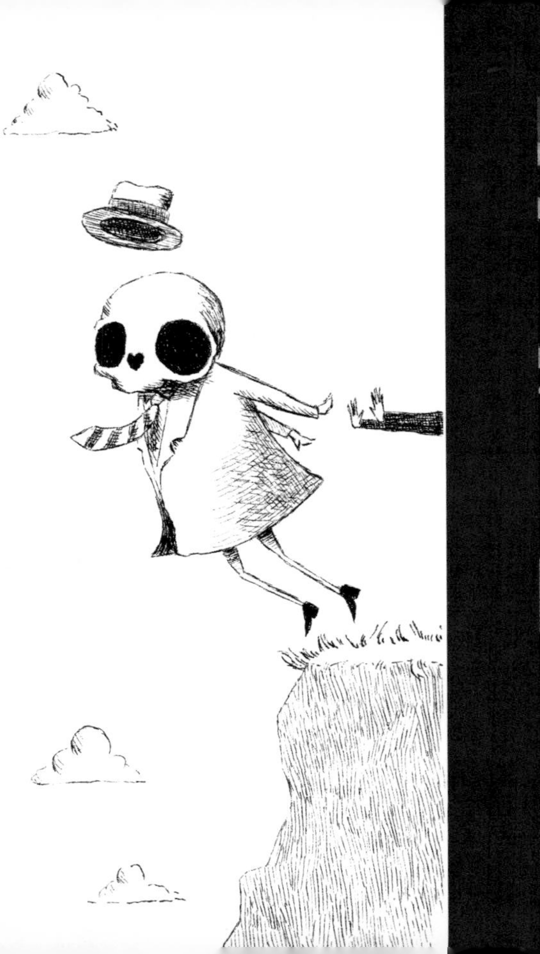

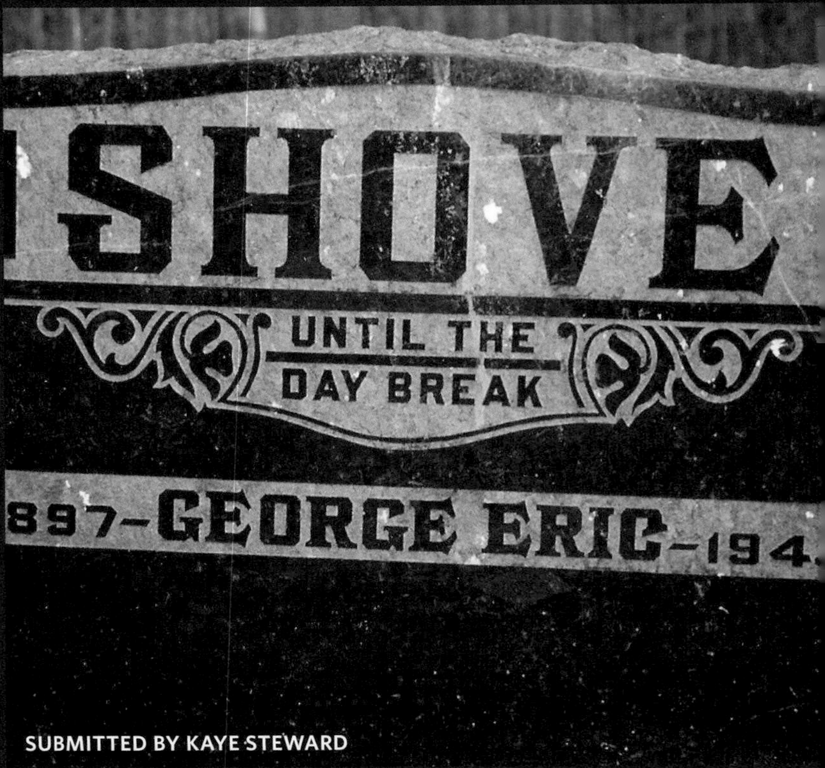
SHOVE
UNTIL THE
DAY BREAK
897-GEORGE ERIC-194

SUBMITTED BY KAYE STEWARD

PUSH CAME.

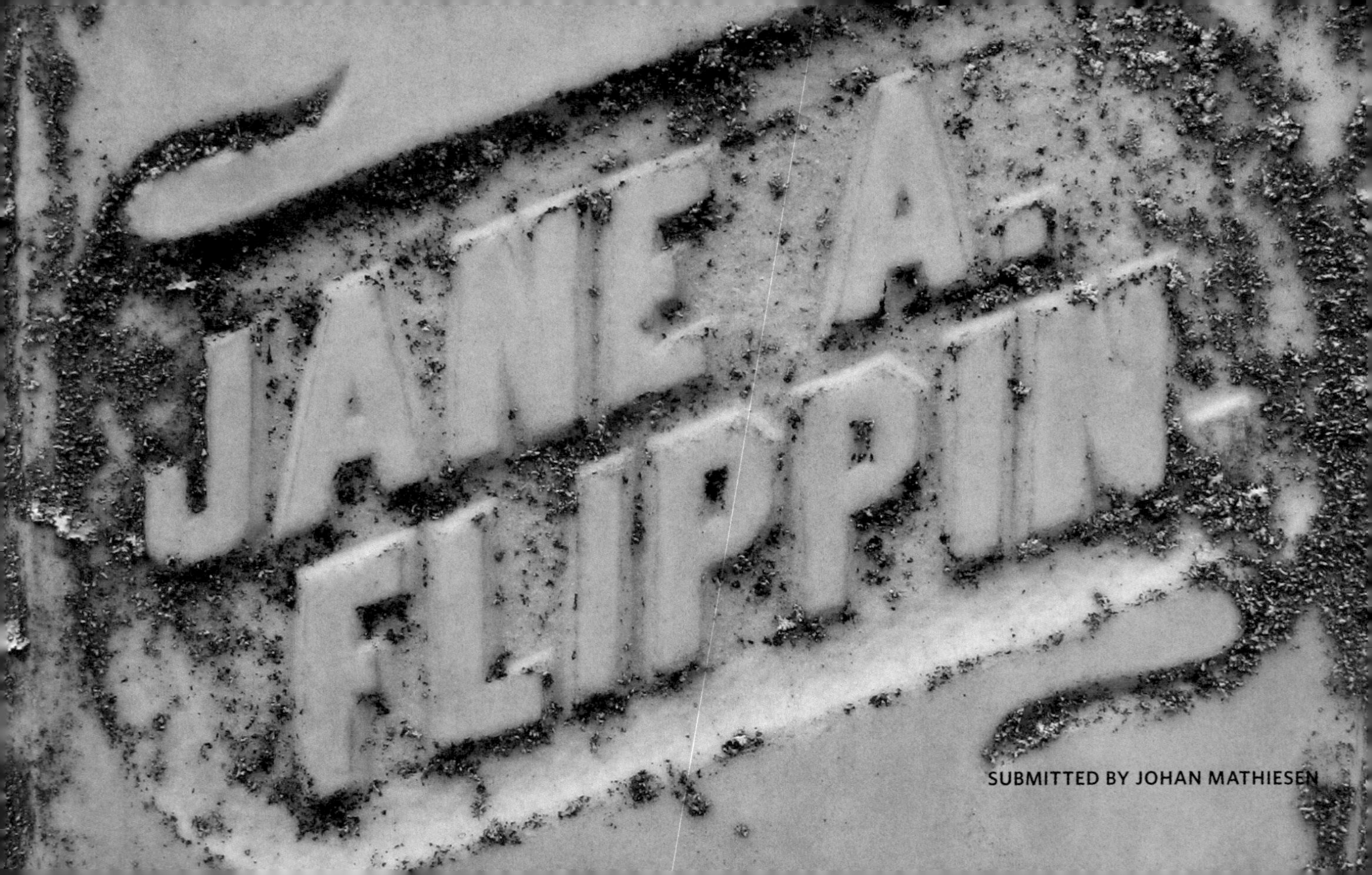
JANE A.
FLIPPIN

SUBMITTED BY JOHAN MATHIESEN

Jane was ALWAYS a rabble-rouser.

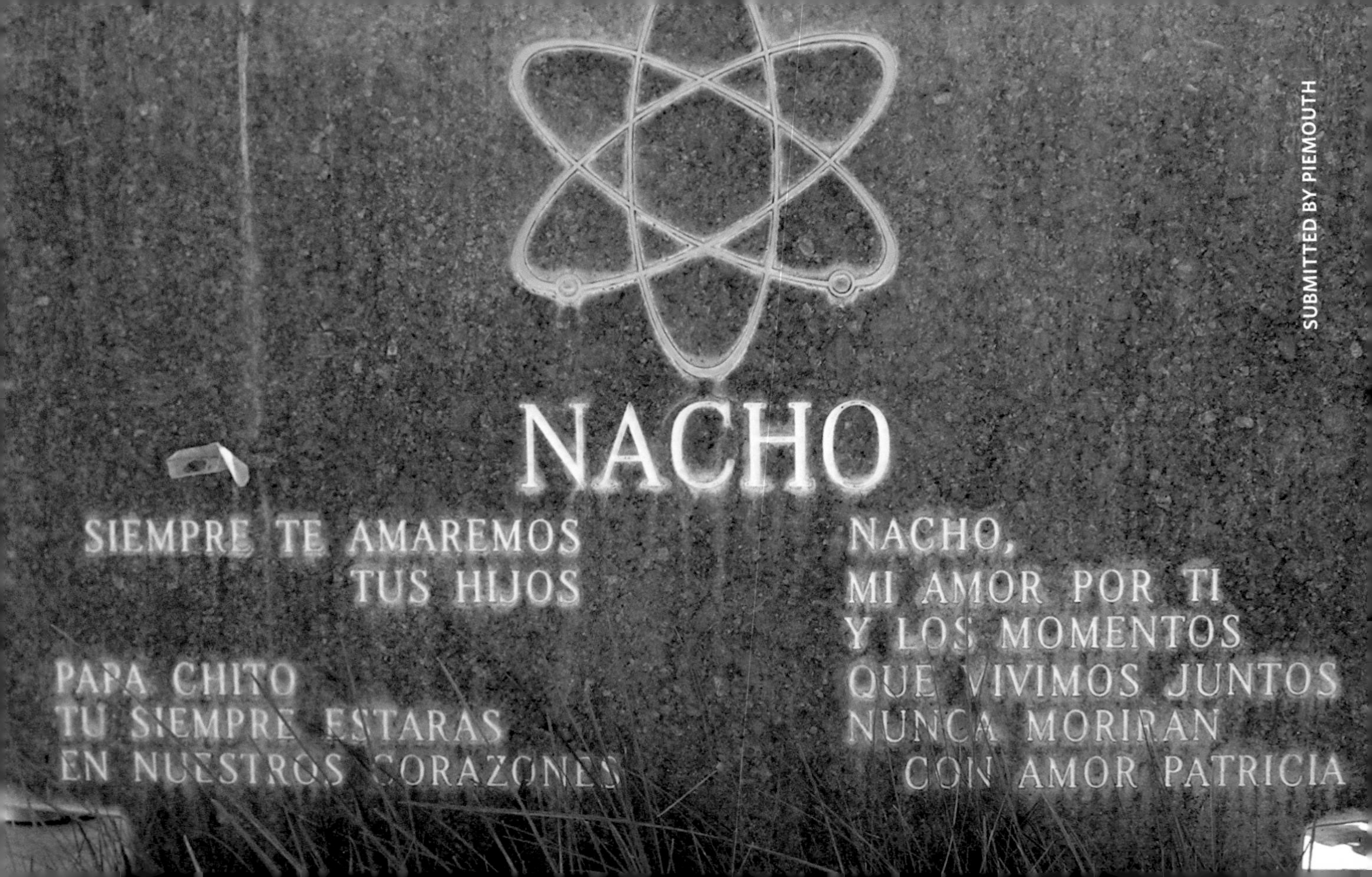
NACHO
SIEMPRE TE AMAREMOS
TUS HIJOS
PAPA CHITO
TU SIEMPRE ESTARAS
EN NUESTROS CORAZONES
NACHO,
MI AMOR POR TI
Y LOS MOMENTOS
QUE VIVIMOS JUNTOS
NUNCA MORIRAN
CON AMOR PATRICIA
SUBMITTED BY PIEMOUTH

Yo, quiero más nachos!

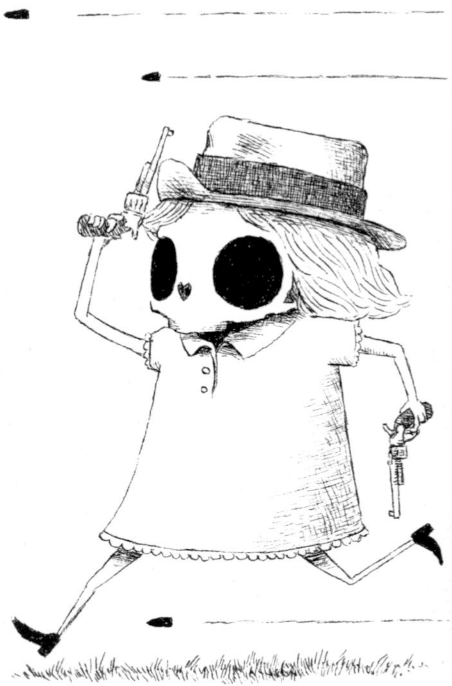

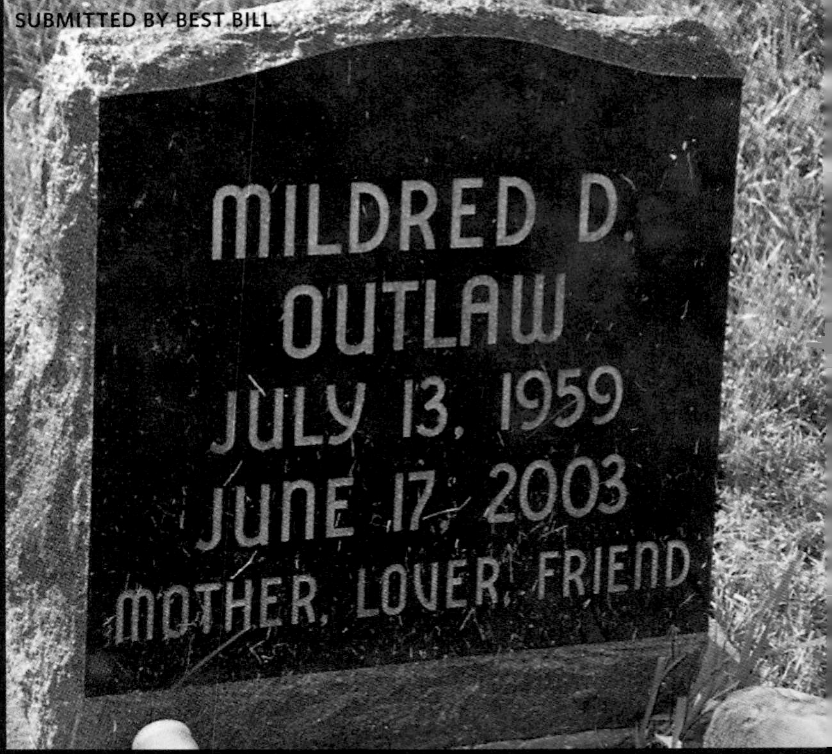
MILDRED D.
OUTLAW
JULY 13, 1959
JUNE 17, 2003
MOTHER, LOVER, FRIEND

SUBMITTED BY BEST BILL

They'd never take her
ALIVE!

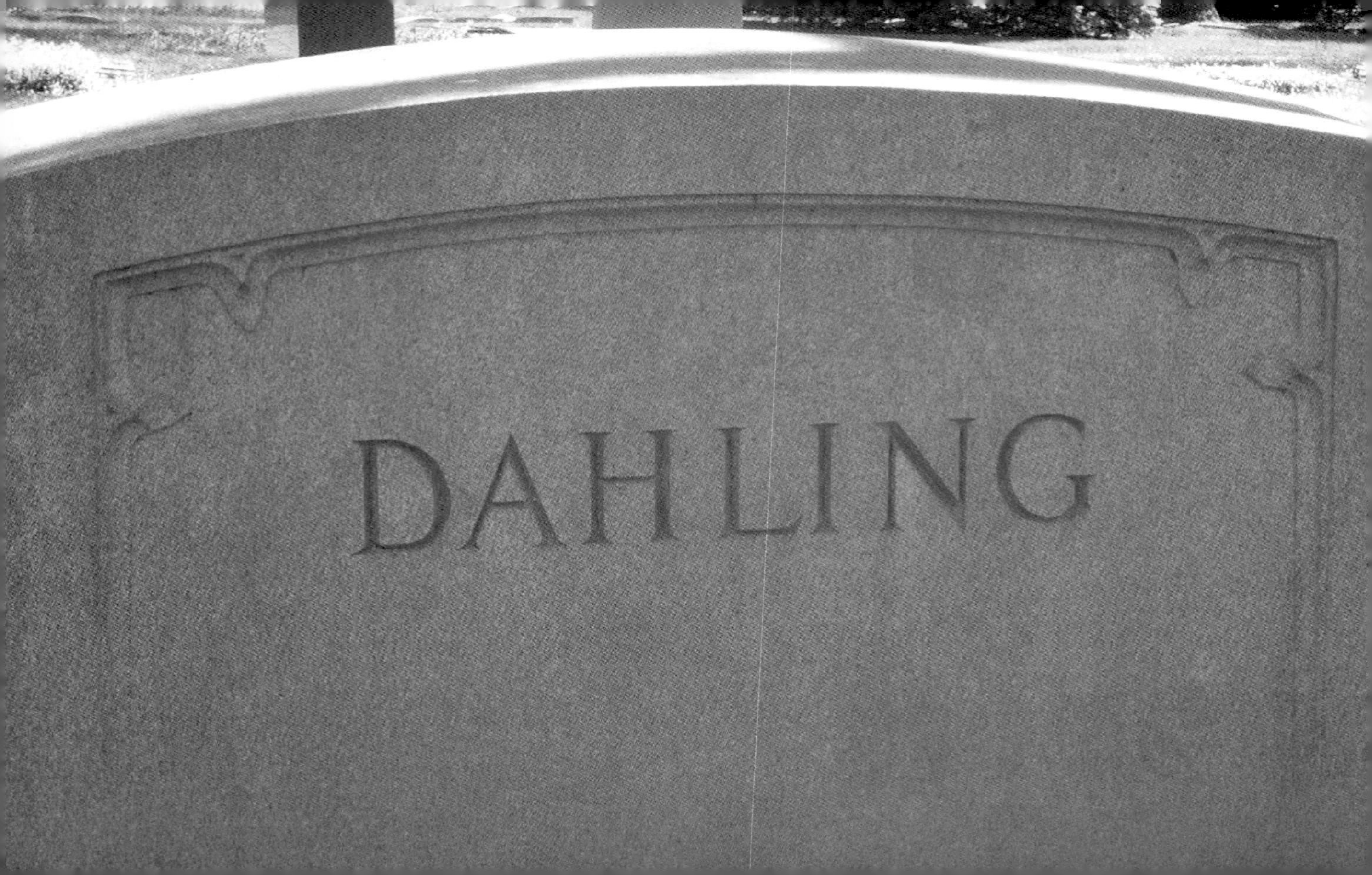
DAHLING

That gravestone is

DIVINE.

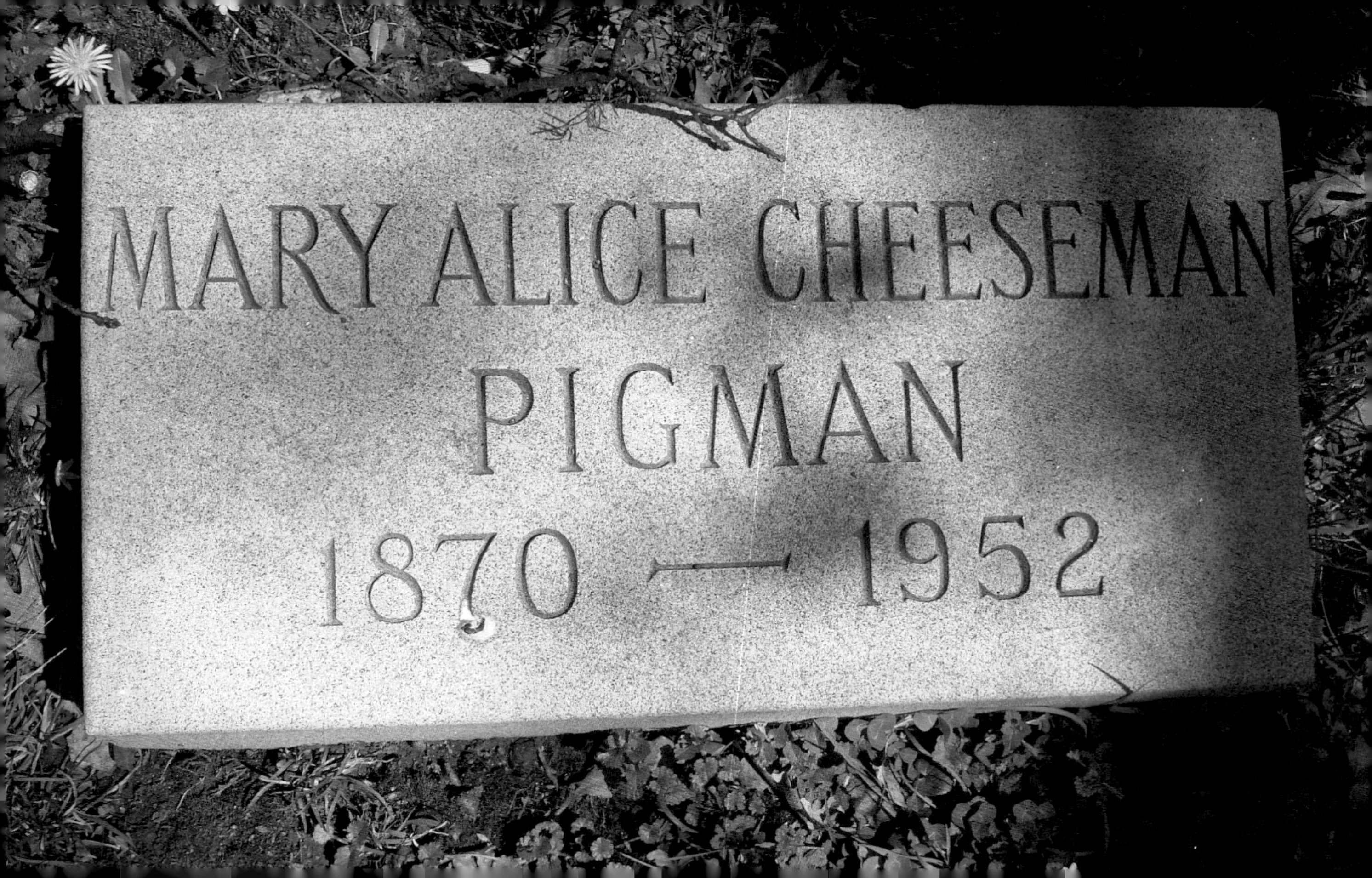
MARY ALICE CHEESEMAN
PIGMAN
1870 — 1952

She married into the

WRONG

family.

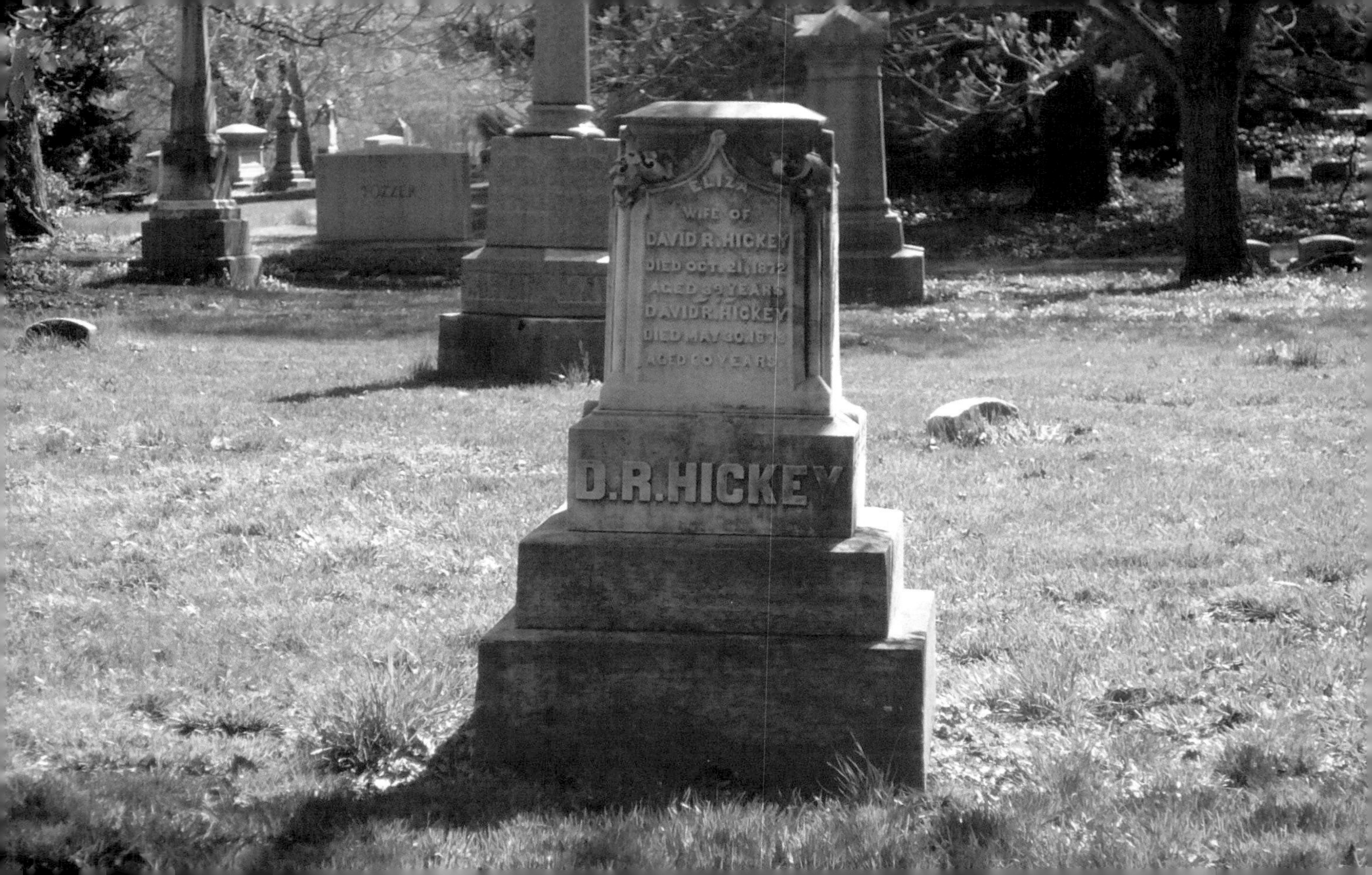
ELIZA
WIFE OF
DAVID R. HICKEY
DIED OCT. 21, 1872
DAVID R. HICKEY
D.R.HICKEY

He wants to be **YOUR** primary care provider.

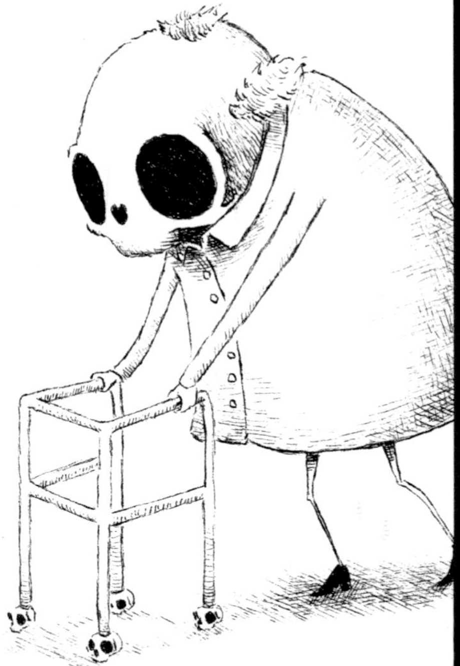

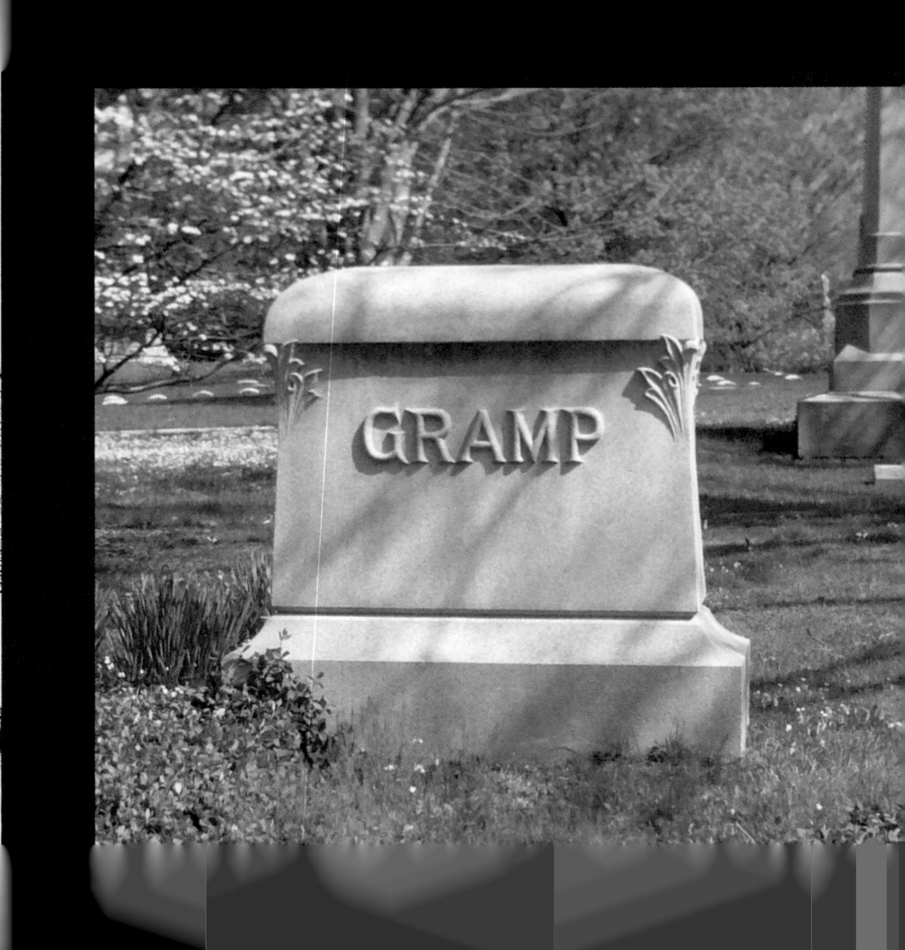
GRAMP

He's a descendant of the Walkers.

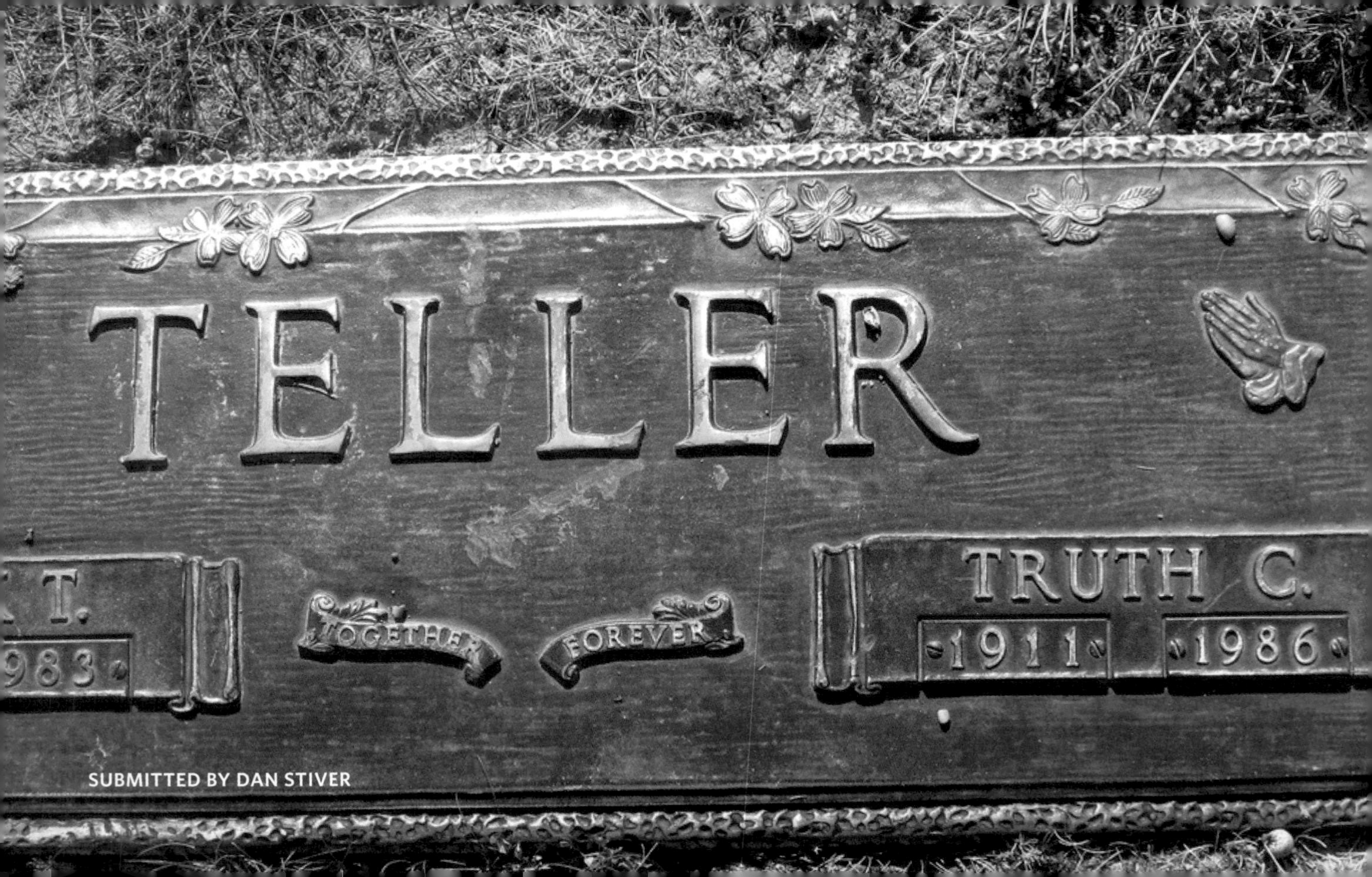
TELLER
T.
983
TOGETHER
FOREVER
TRUTH C.
1911
1986
SUBMITTED BY DAN STIVER

Q: When does a truth-teller lie?

A: When she's dead.

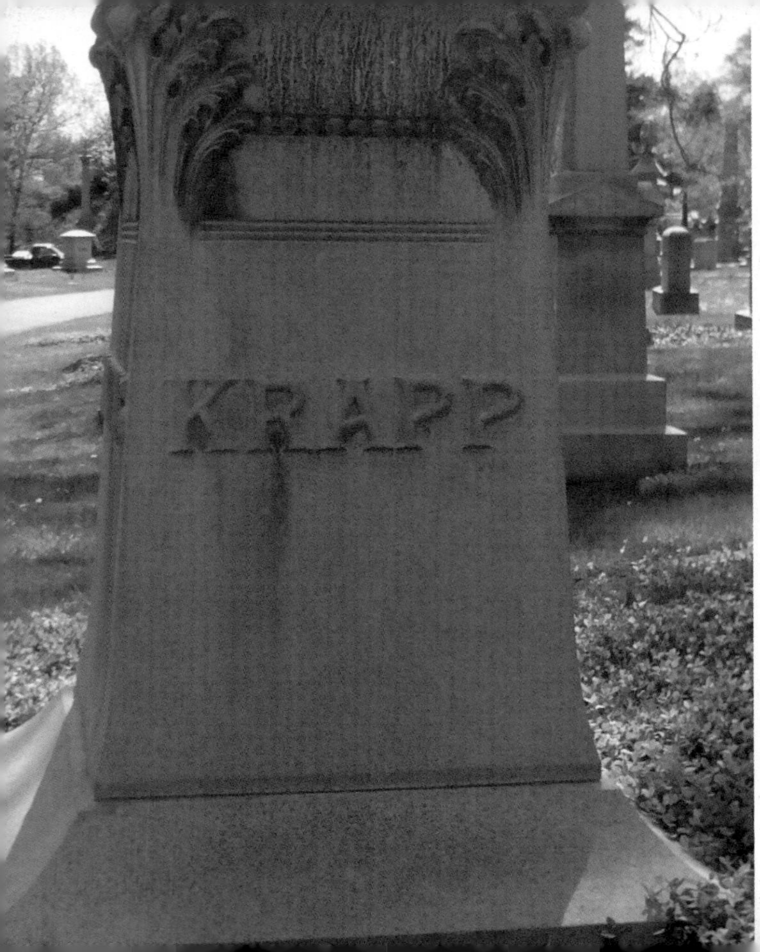
KRAPP
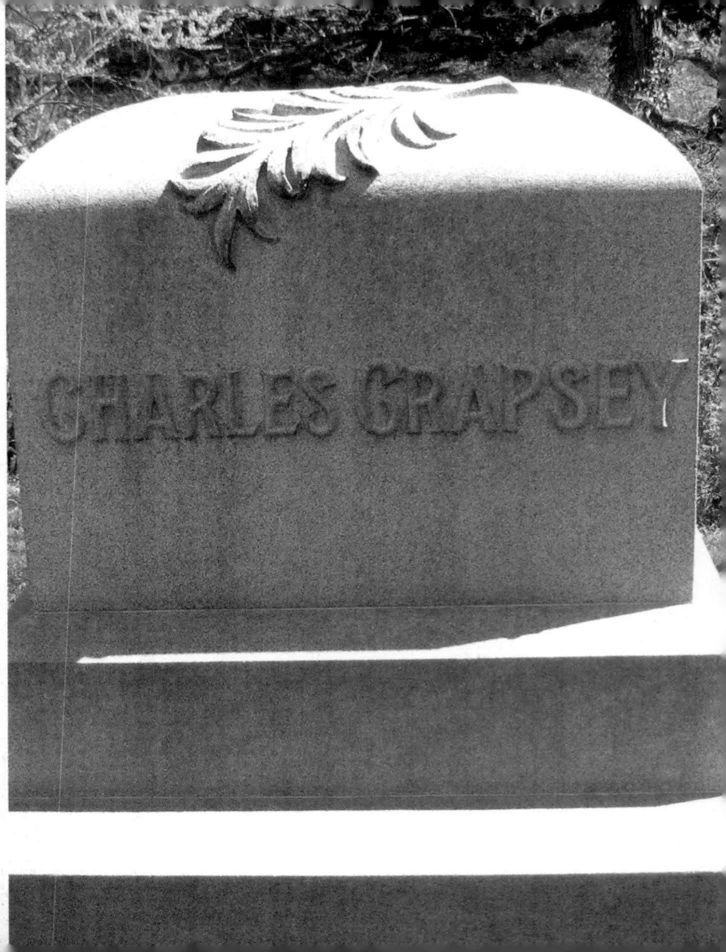
CHARLES GRAPSEY

No matter how you spell it, it still STINKS.

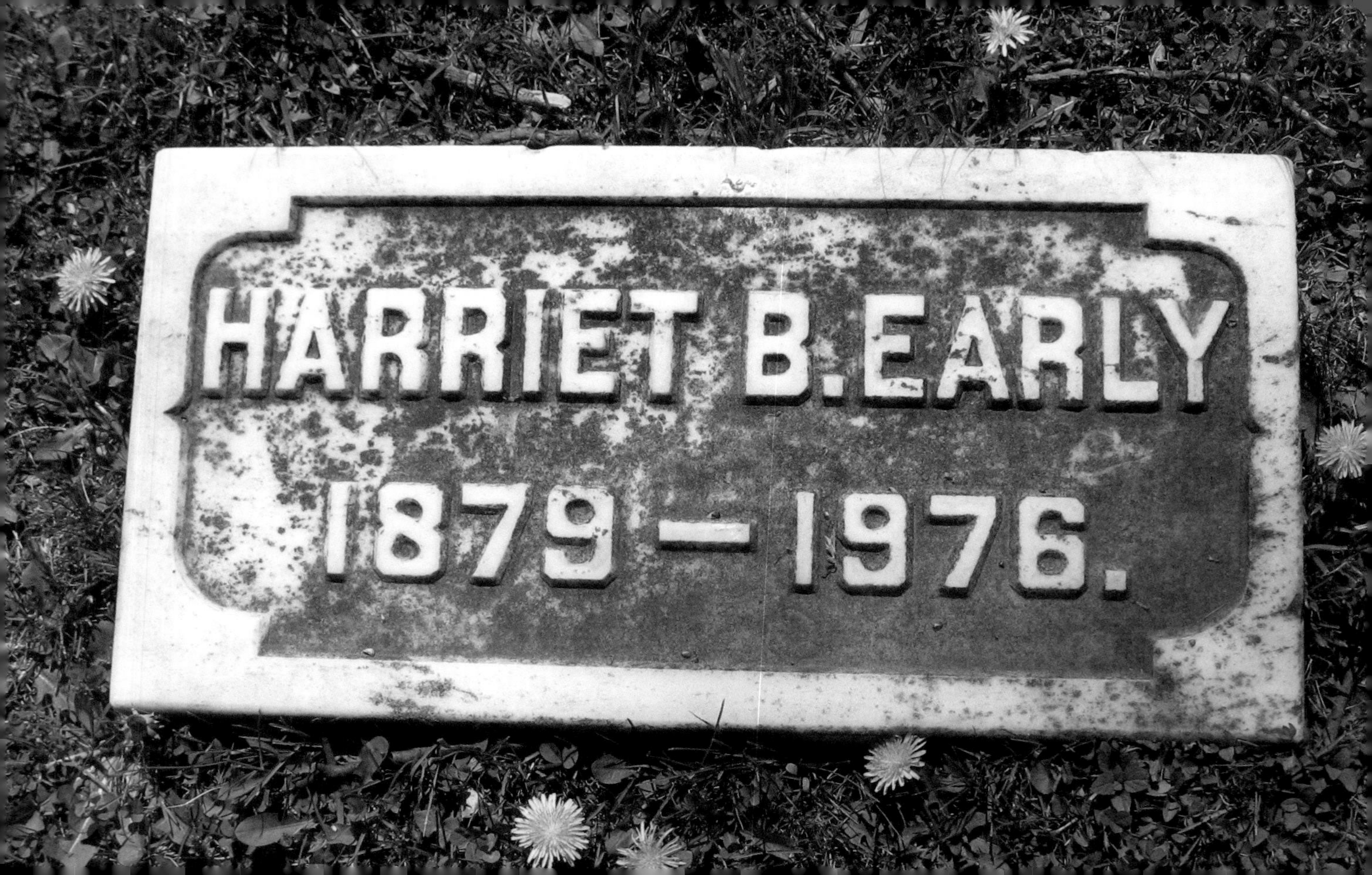
HARRIET B. EARLY
1879 — 1976.

Now she's late.

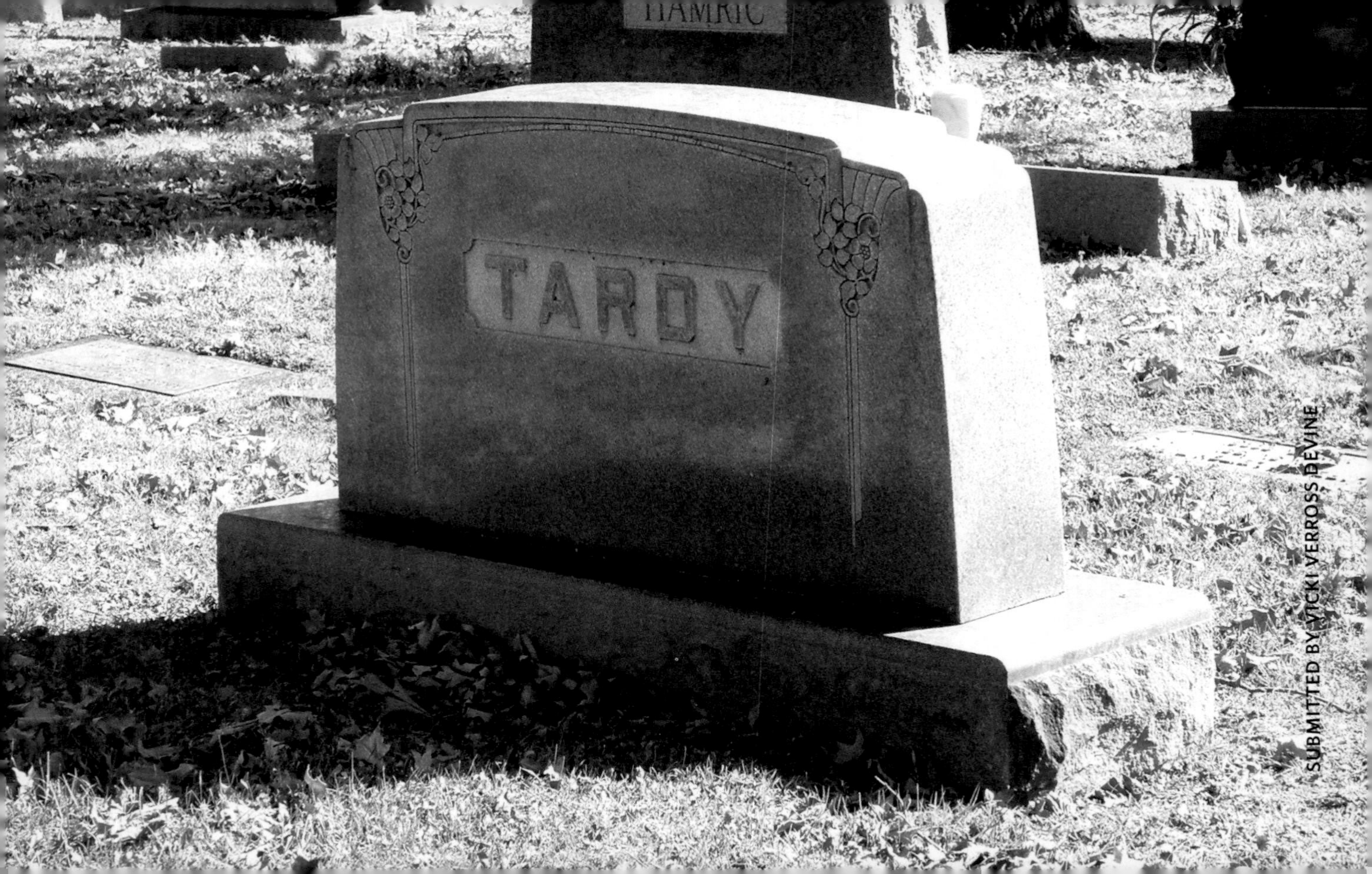
TARDY

SUBMITTED BY VICKI VERROSS DEVINE

Better late than never.

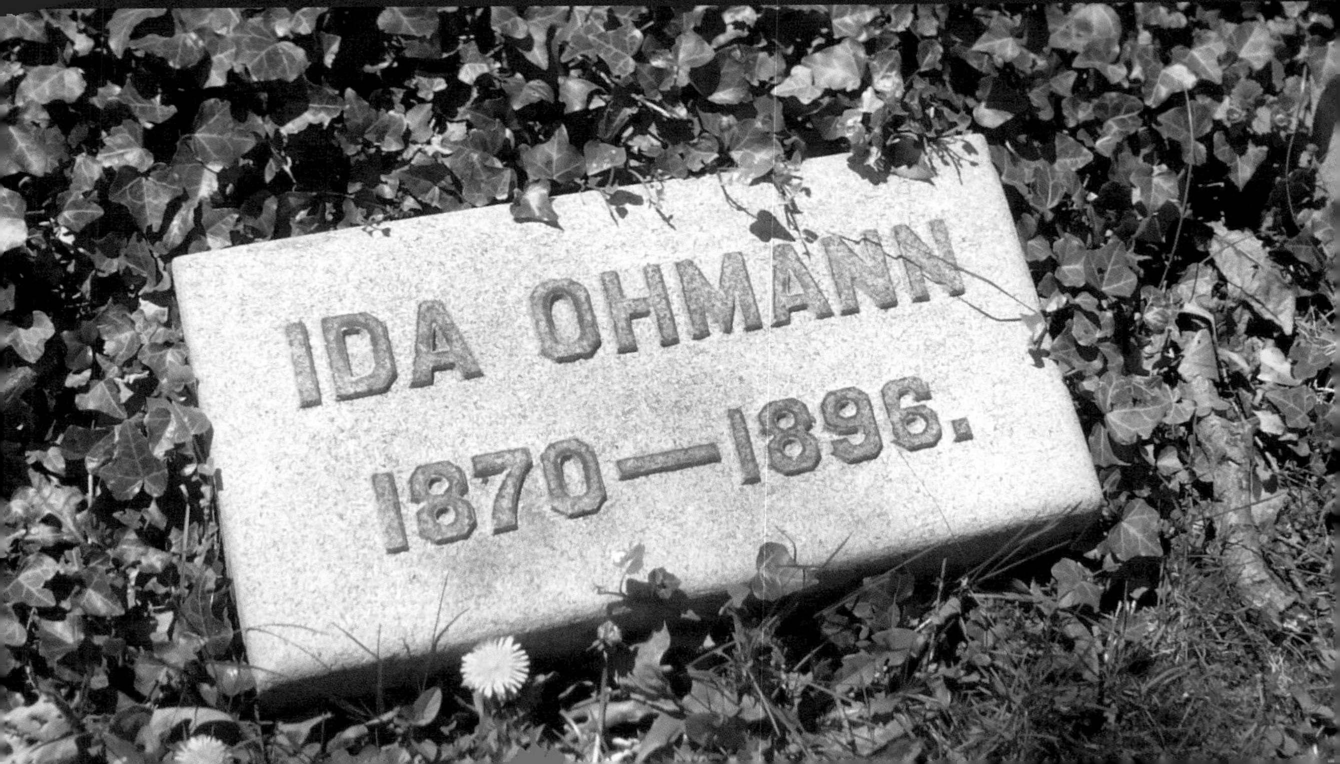
IDA OHMANN
1870—1896.

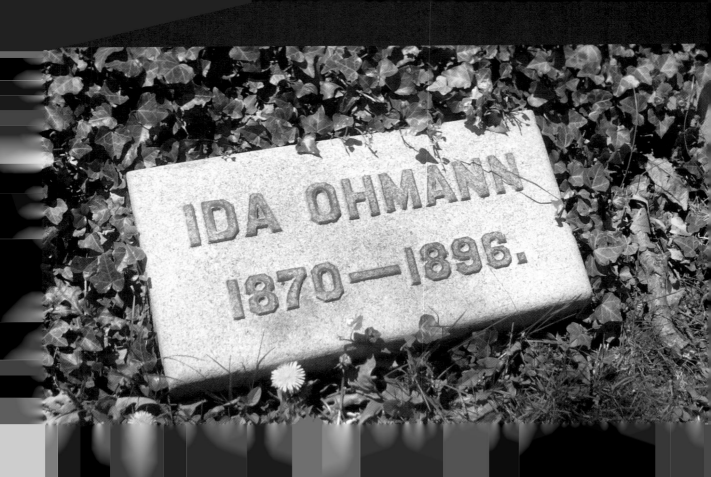

D'oh!!!

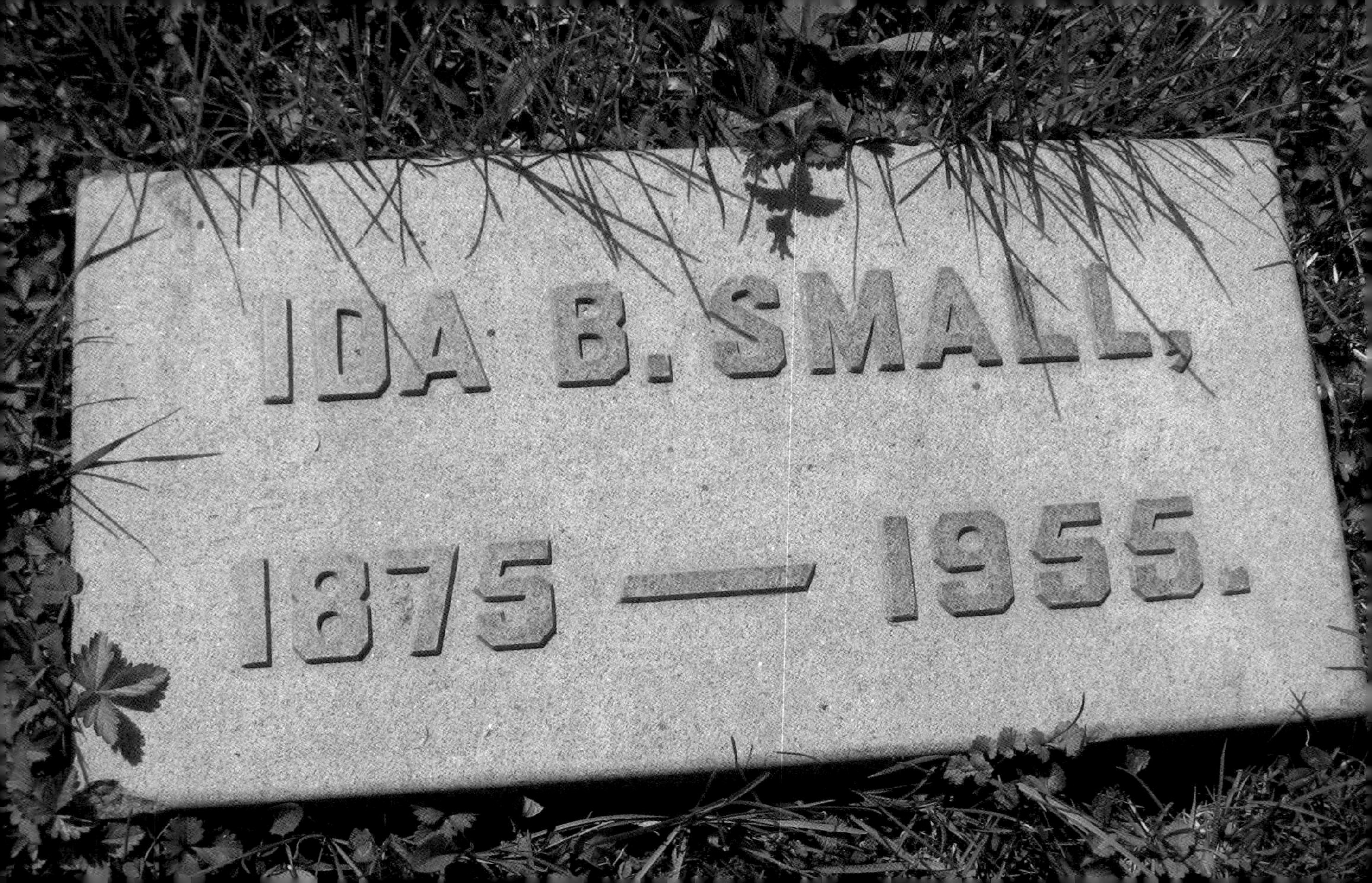
IDA B. SMALL,
1875 — 1955.

IDA DREW THE SHORT STRAW.

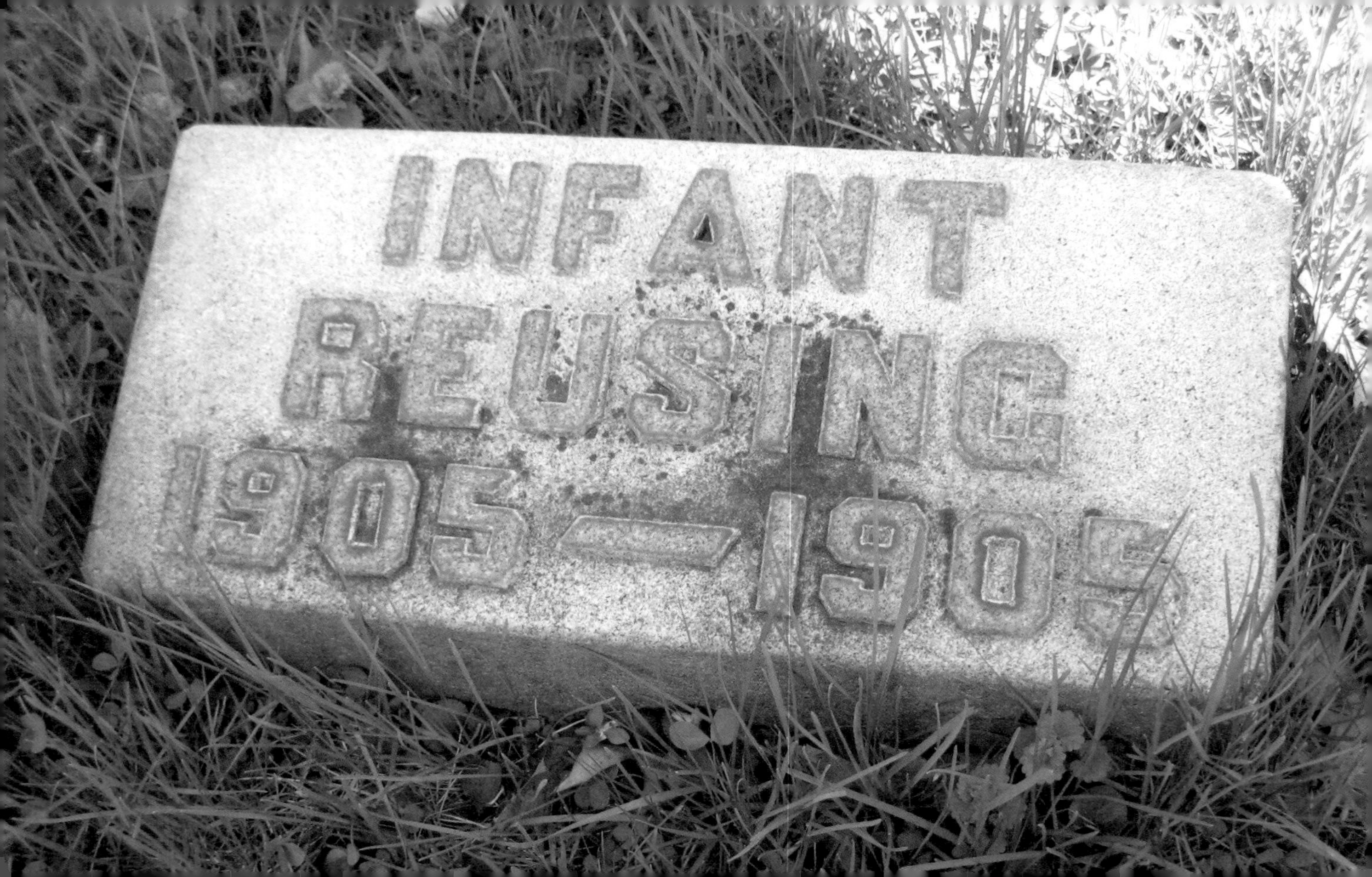
INFANT
REUSING
1905–1905

Recycling gone TOO far

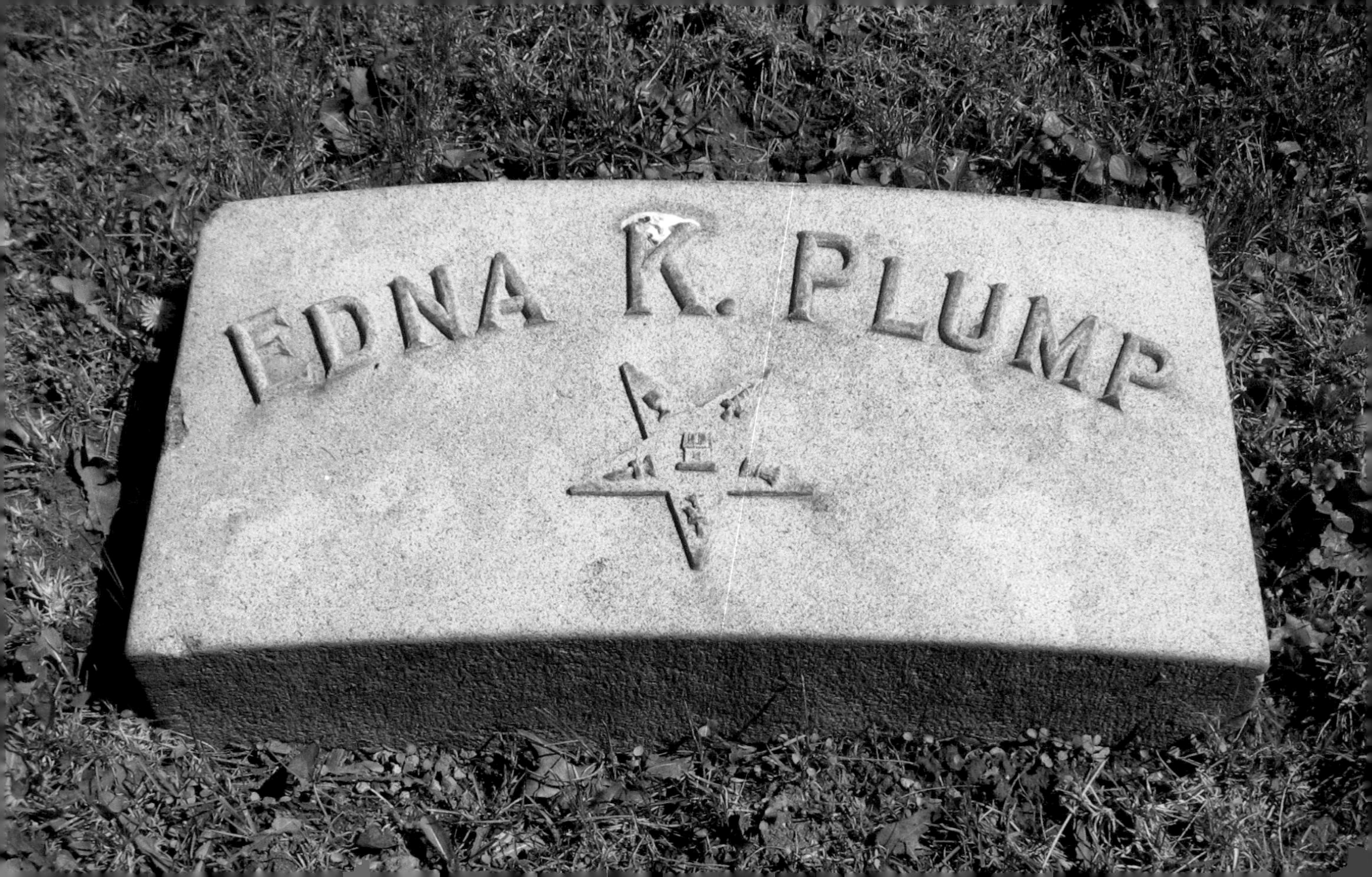
EDNA K. PLUMP

She's not fat, just

BIG
boned.

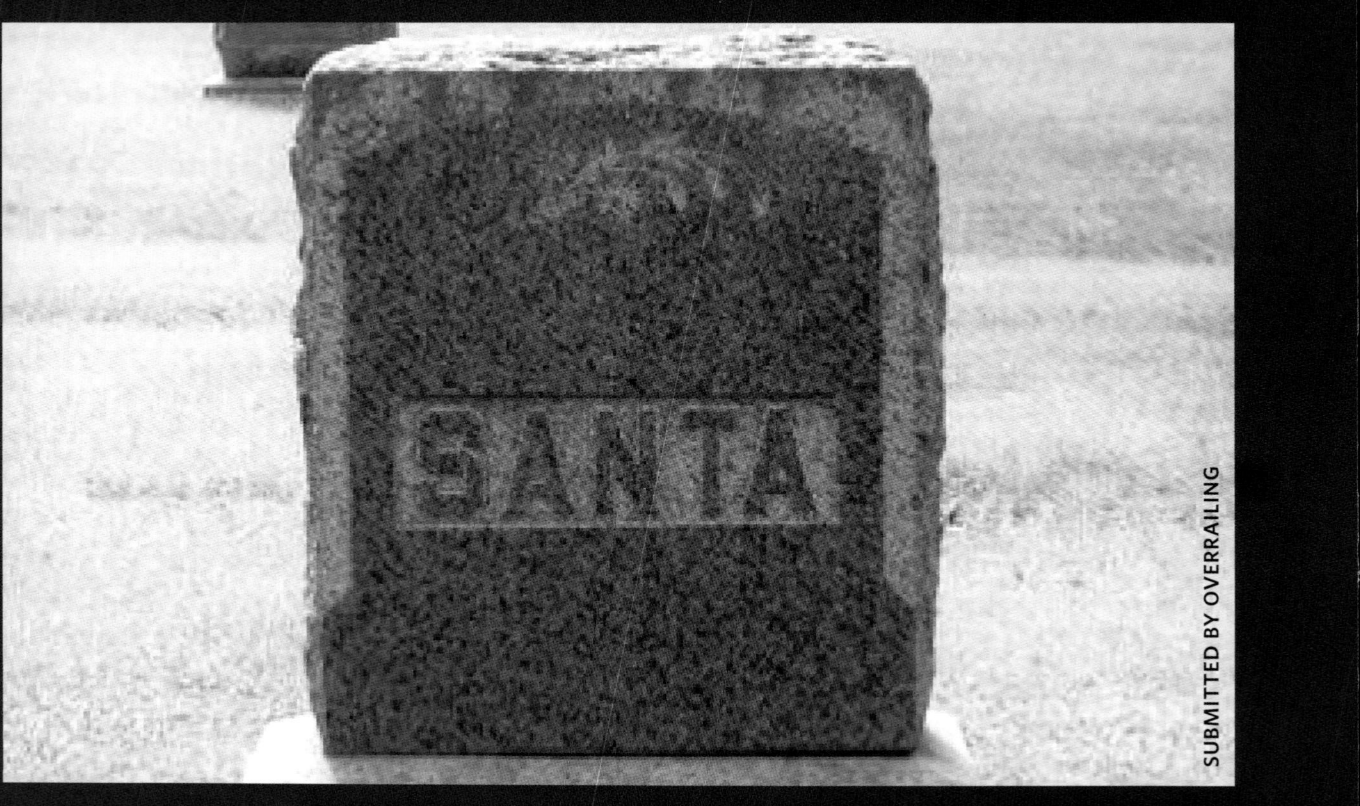
SANTA

SUBMITTED BY OVERRAILING

Mrs. Claus told him not to use off-brand reins.

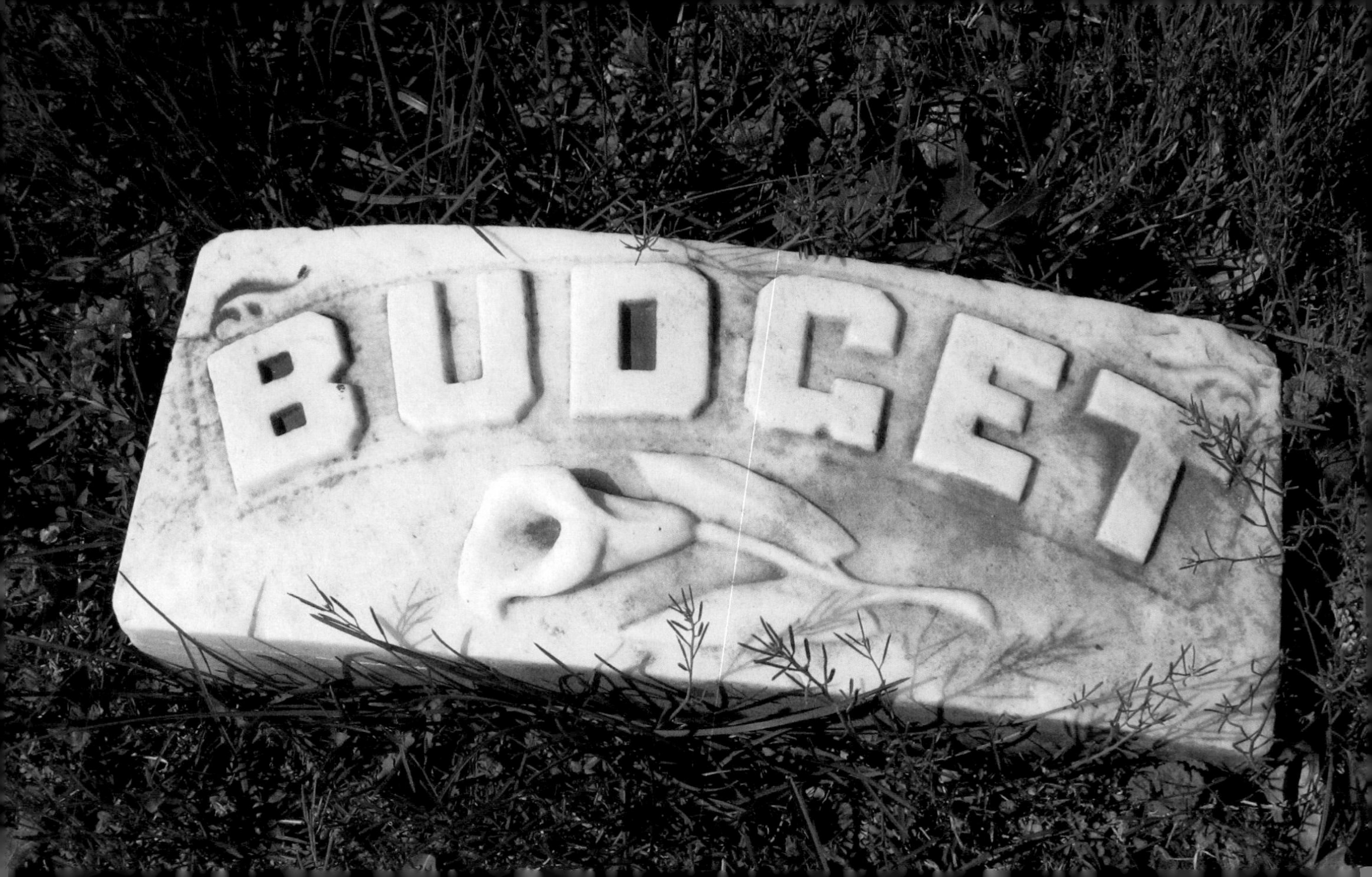
BUDGET

NEVER EVER

miss your numbers.

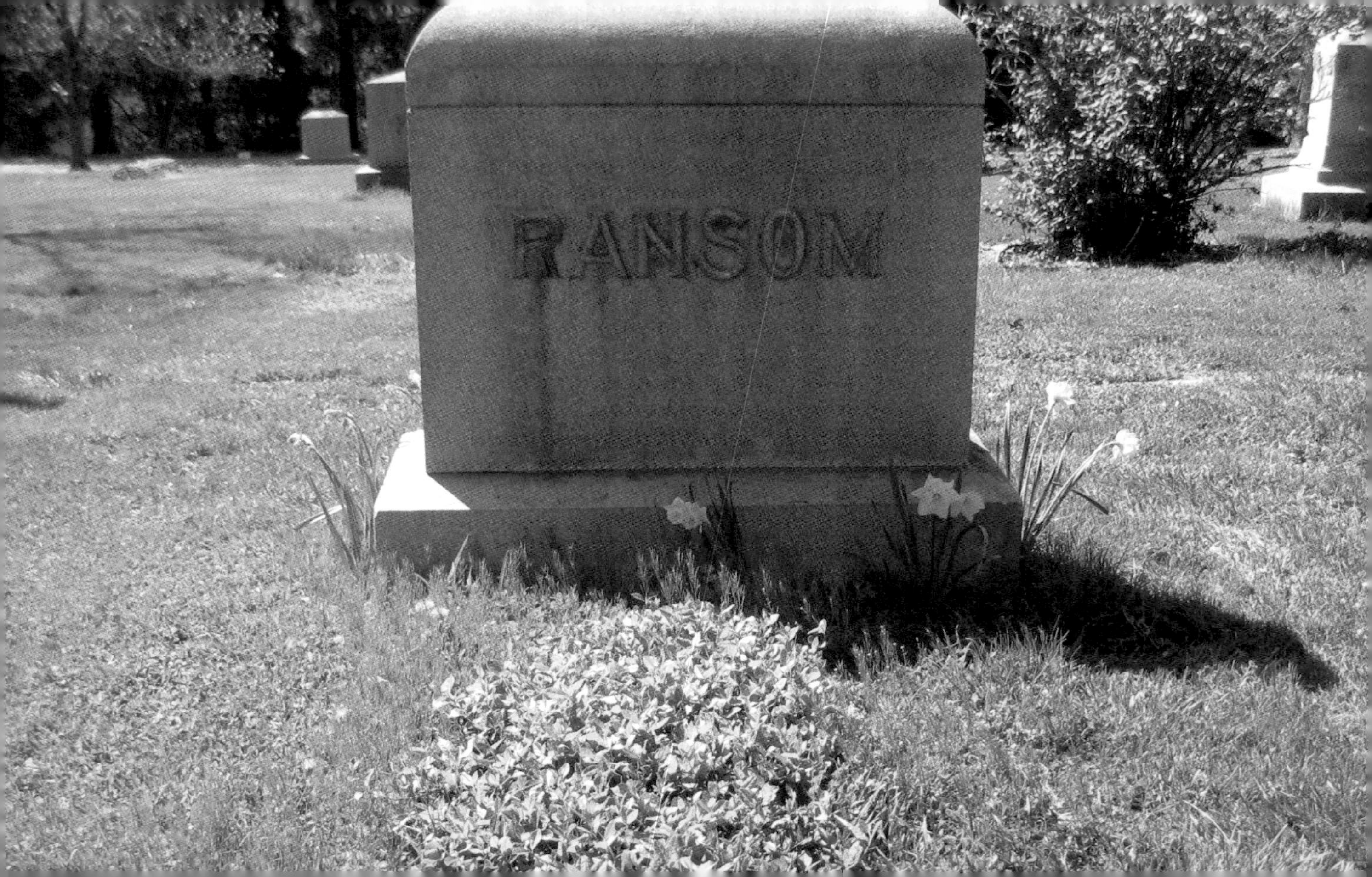
RANSOM

They misunderstood the kidnapper's instructions.

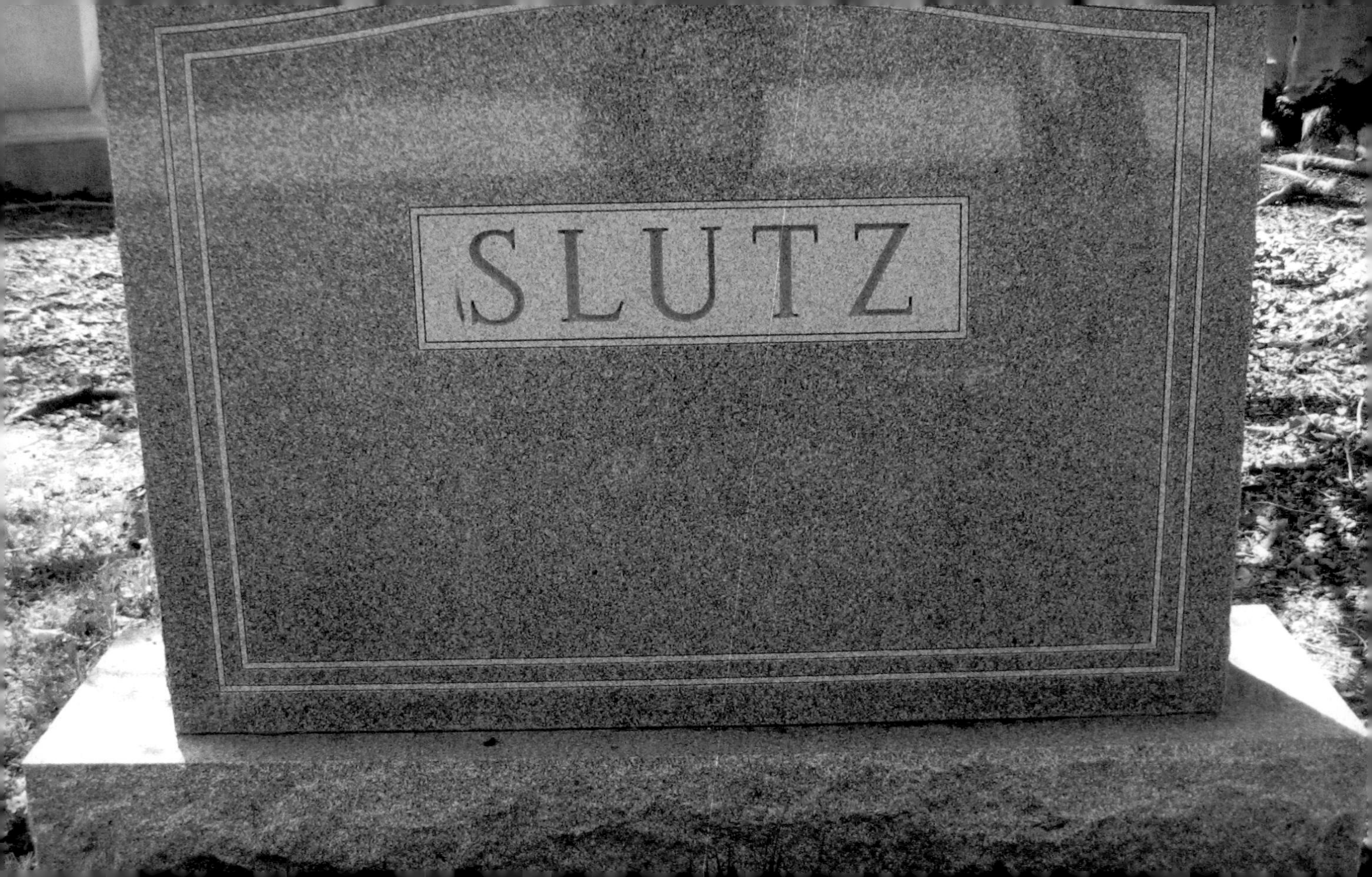
SLUTZ

Easy come, easy go.

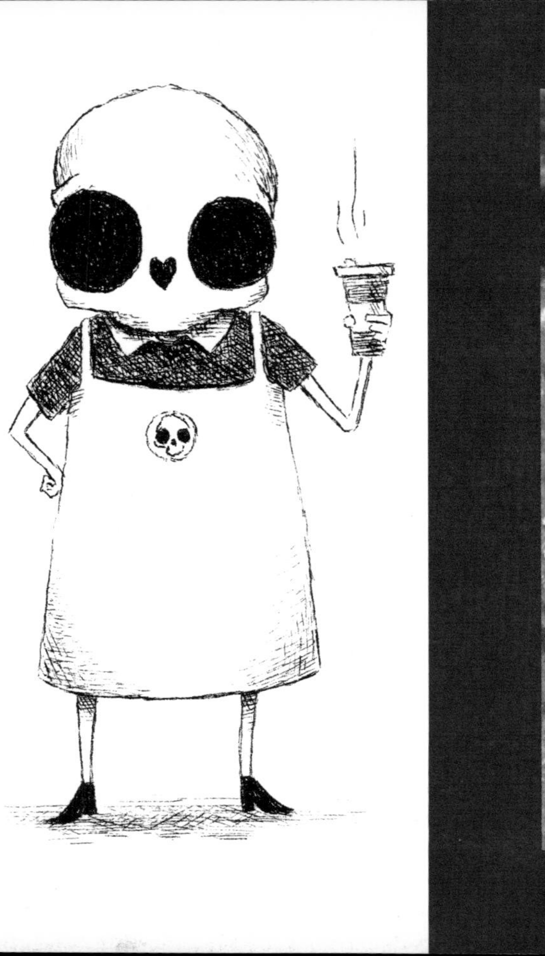

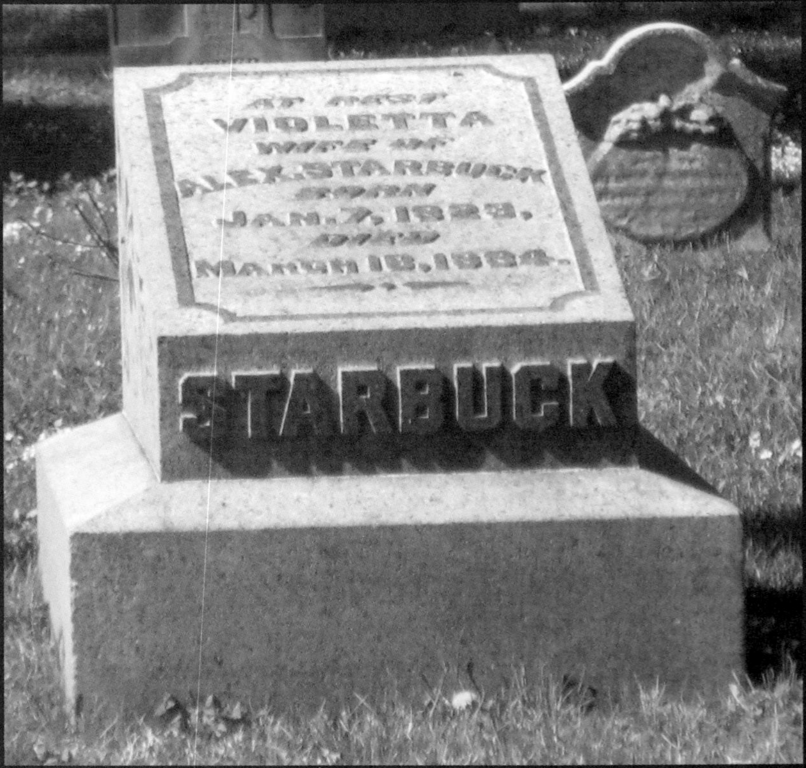
VIOLETTA
ALEX.STARBUCK
STARBUCK

Should've made the grave a

VENTI.

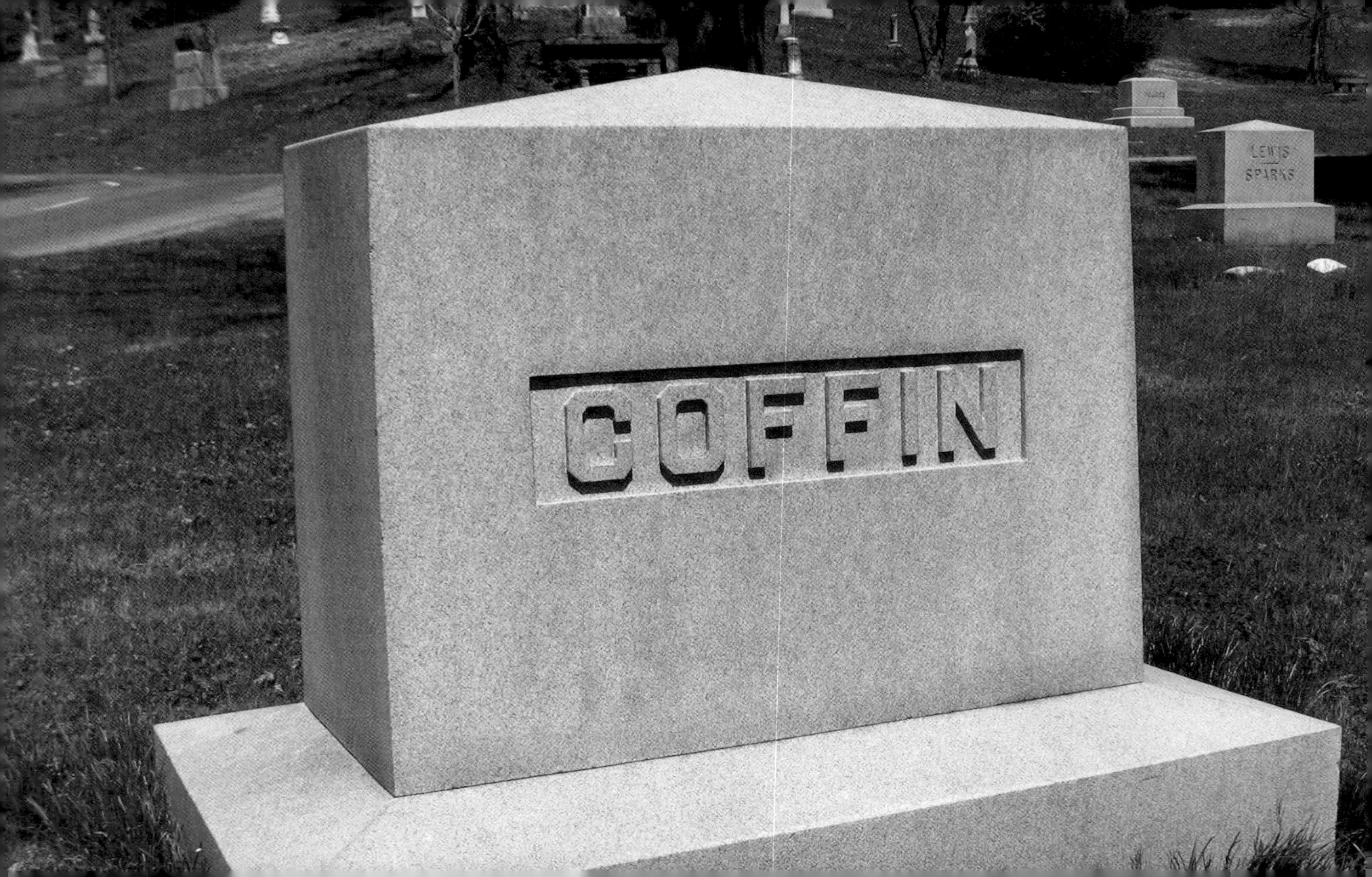
COFFIN
LEWIS
SPARKS

Yes, but what's IN it?

MOM??

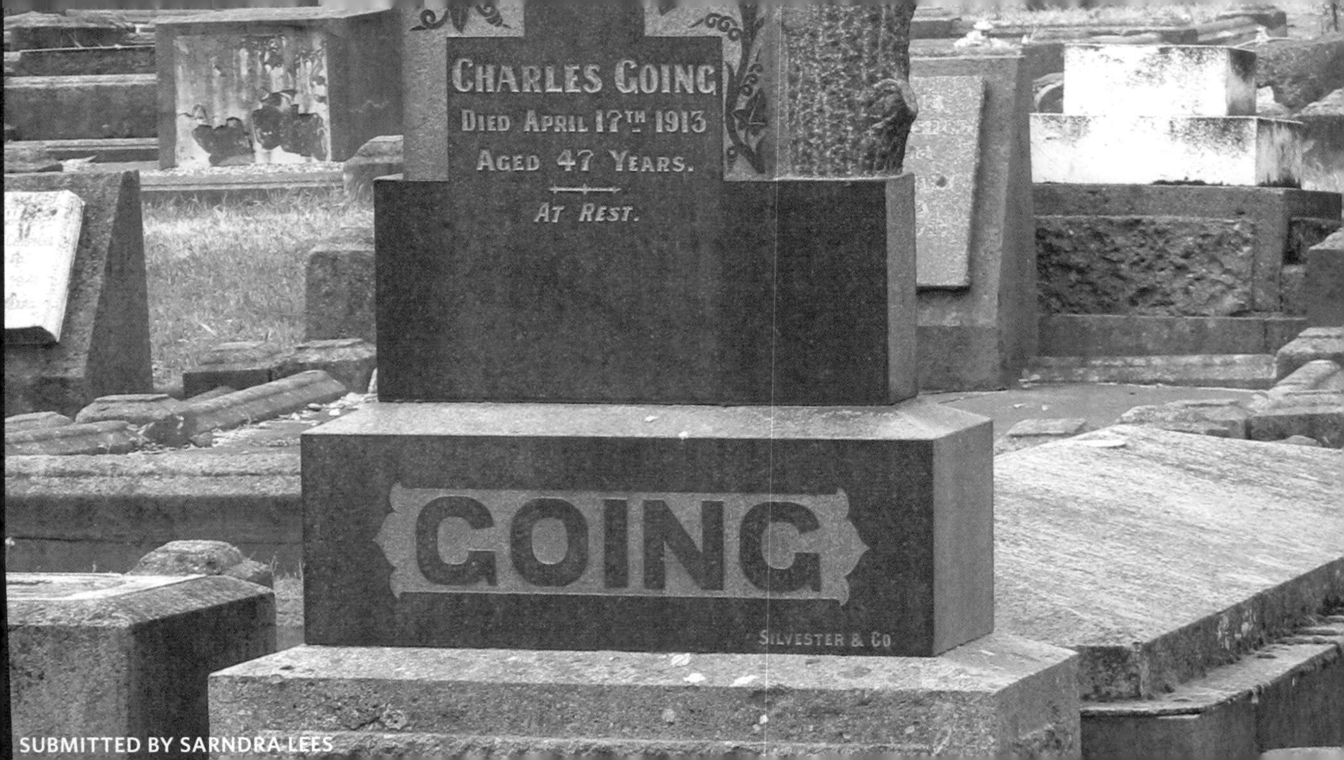

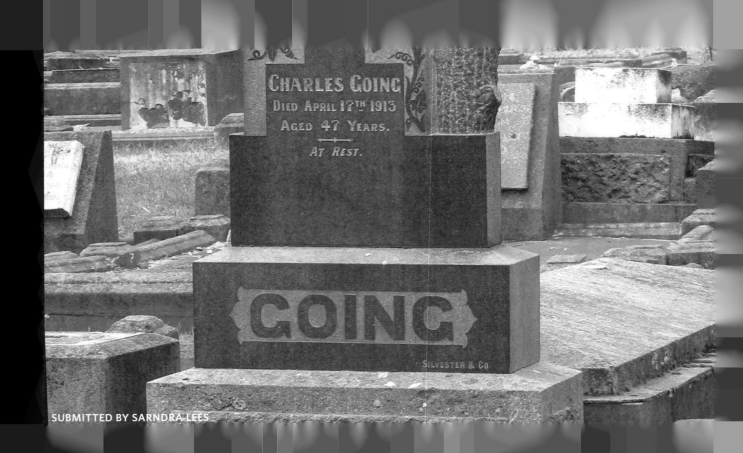

CHARLES GOING
DIED APRIL 17TH 1913
AGED 47 YEARS.
AT REST.
GOING
SILVESTER & CO

SUBMITTED BY SARNDRA LEES

GOING, GONE

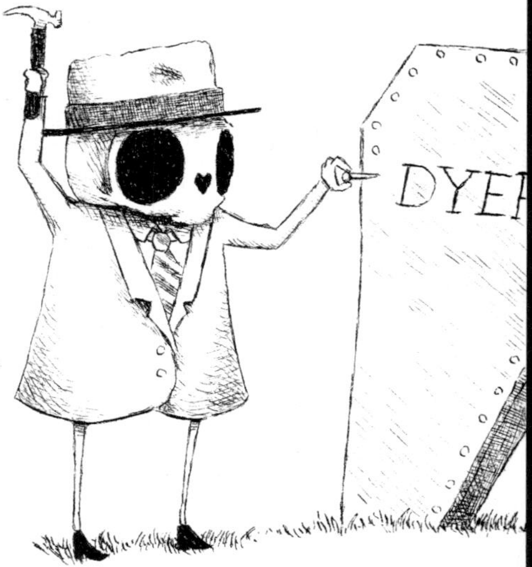

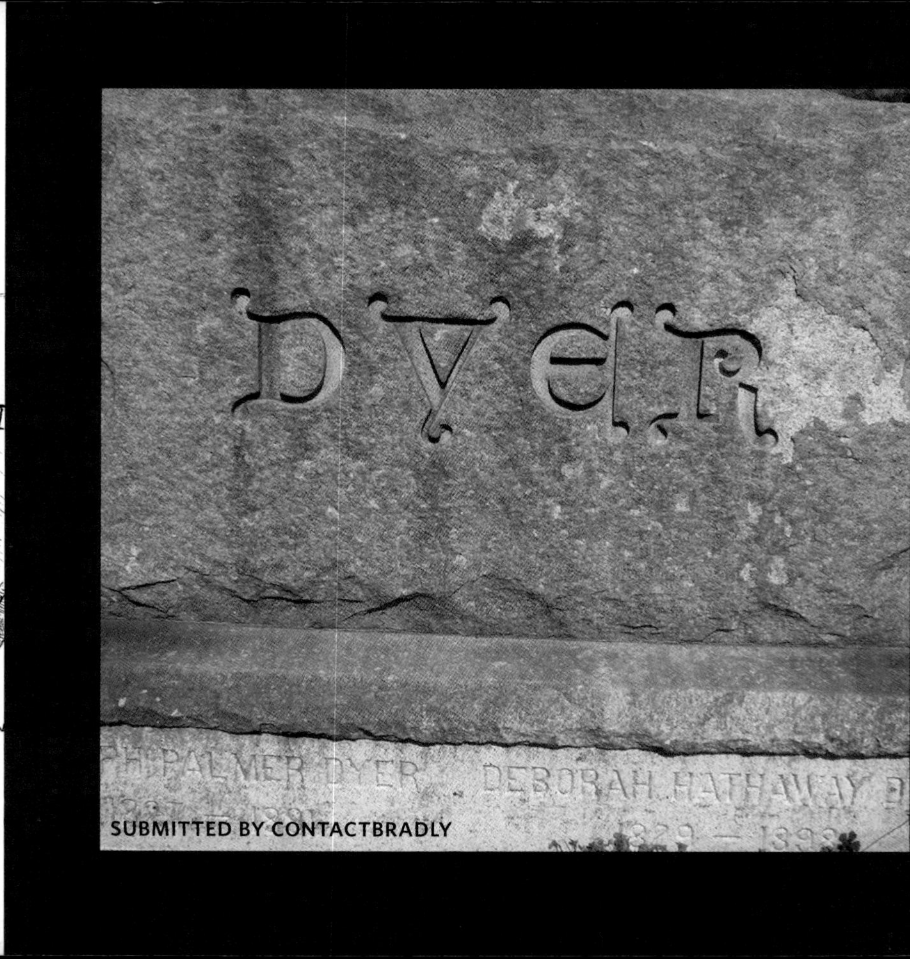
DYER
PALMER DYER
DEBORAH HATHAWAY

SUBMITTED BY CONTACTBRADLY

We never saw a name **more appropriate** ...

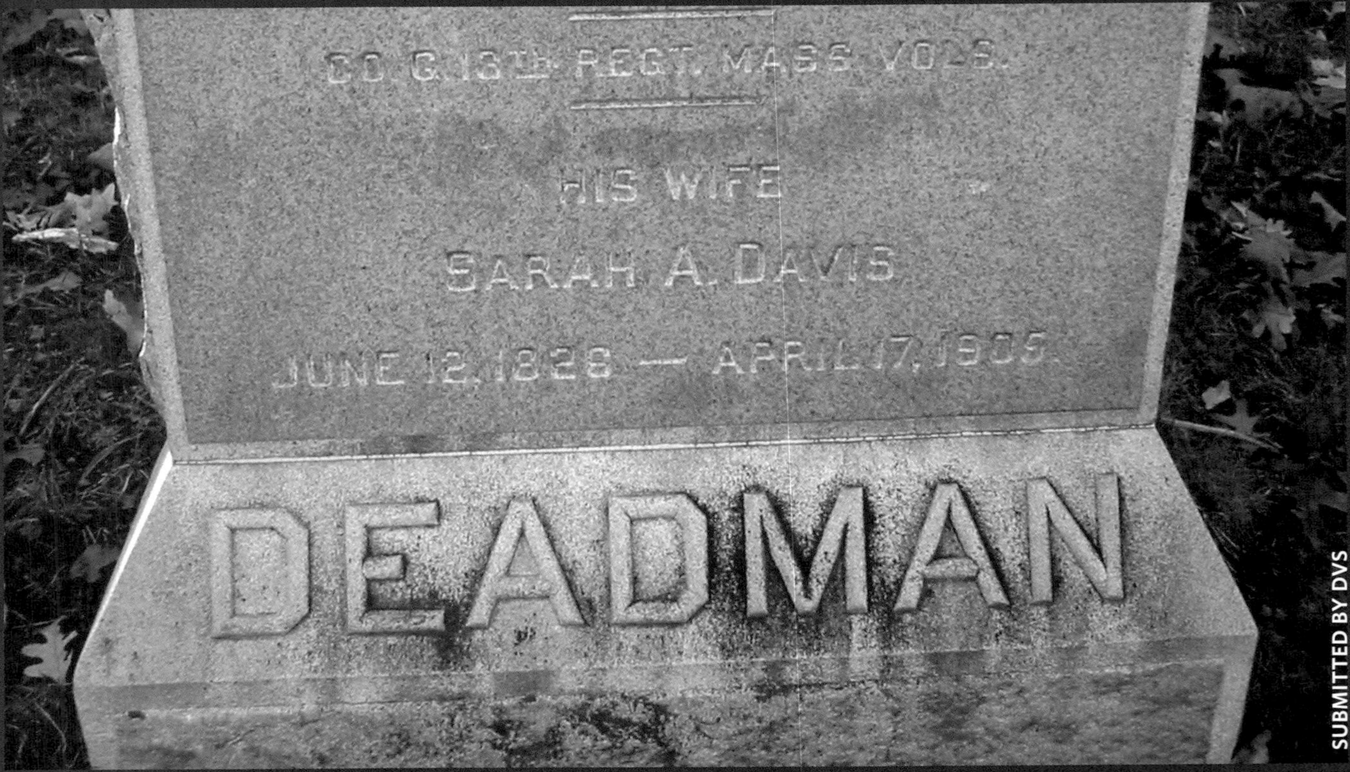
CO. G. 13TH REGT. MASS. VOLS.
HIS WIFE
SARAH A. DAVIS
JUNE 12, 1828 — APRIL 17, 1909
DEADMAN

SUBMITTED BY DVS

... UNTIL NOW.

Download our

Deadly Wallpaper

Go to **<www.gravehumorbook.com>**

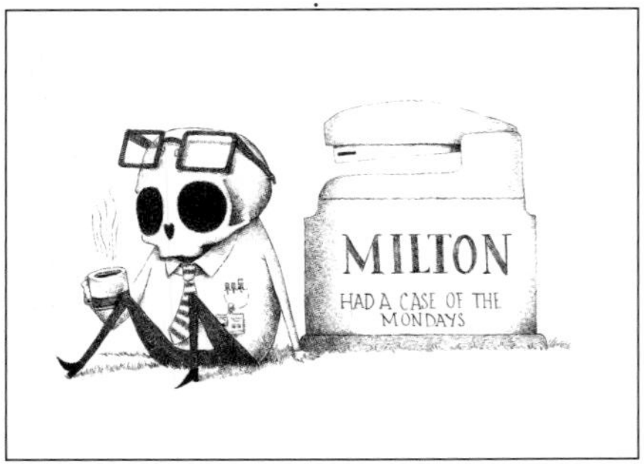
MILTON
HAD A CASE OF THE MONDAYS

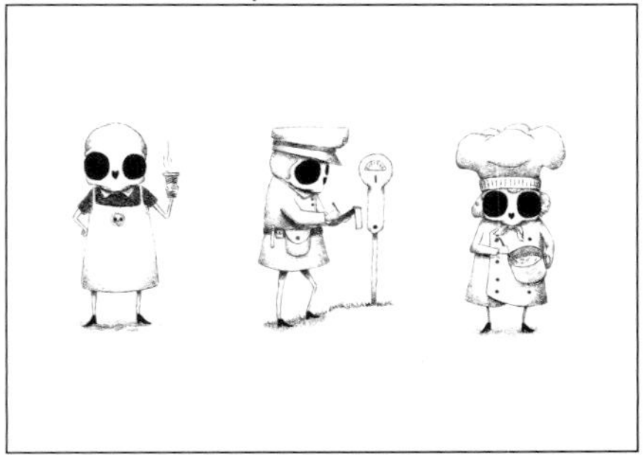

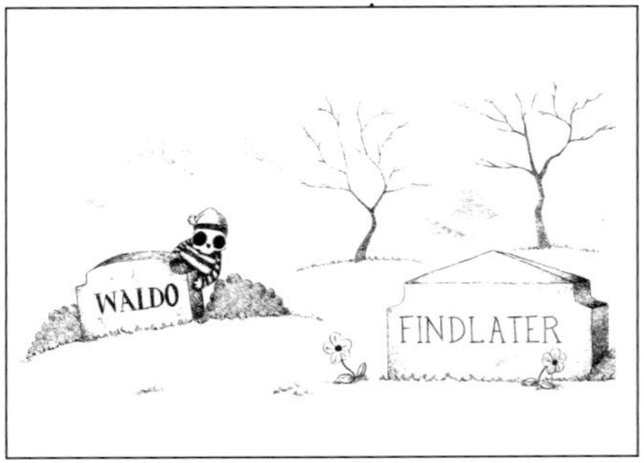
WALDO
FINDLATER

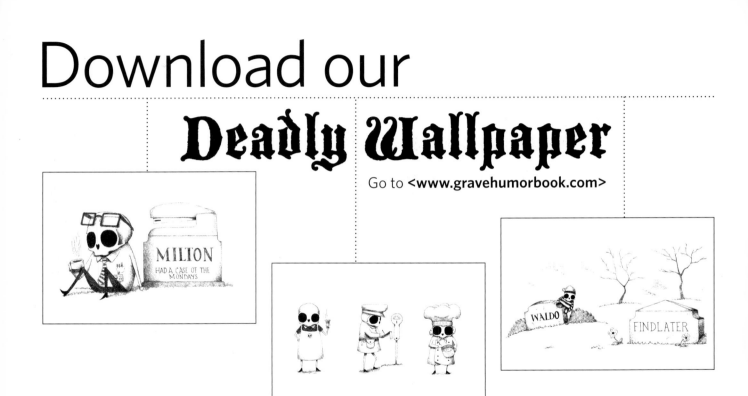

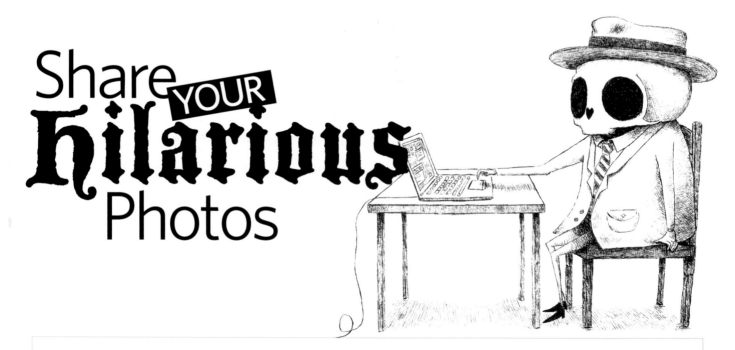

Share YOUR hilarious Photos

Go to <www.gravehumorbook.com>

Tomes from the Crypt

Unearth these and other F+W Media titles at your local bookstore or online bookseller.

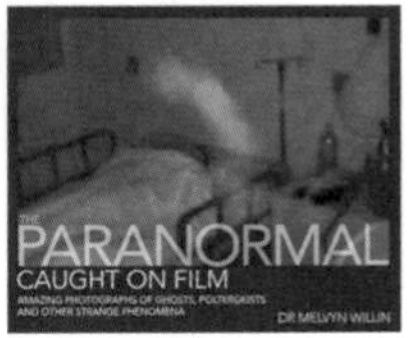
PARANORMAL
CAUGHT ON FILM

THE PARANORMAL CAUGHT ON FILM
By Melvyn Willin

Hardcover

#Z1845

ISBN: 9780715329801

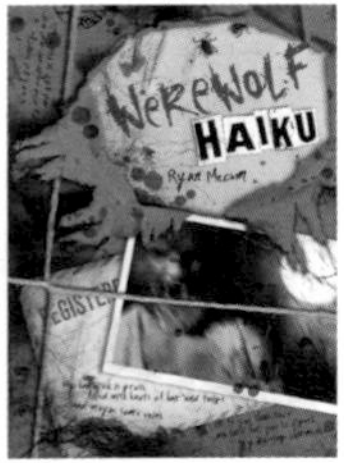
WEREWOLF
HAIKU

WEREWOLF HAIKU
By Ryan Mecum

Paperback

#Z8621

ISBN: 9781440308268

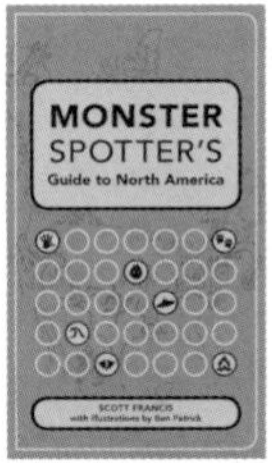
MONSTER
SPOTTER'S
Guide to North America

MONSTER SPOTTER'S GUIDE TO NORTH AMERICA
By Scott Francis with illustrations by Ben Patrick

Paperback

#Z0676

ISBN: 9781581809299

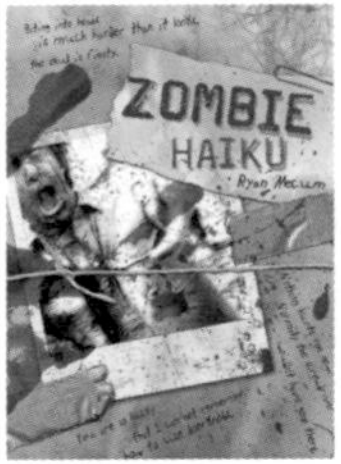
ZOMBIE
HAIKU

ZOMBIE HAIKU
By Ryan Mecum

Paperback

#Z1805

ISBN: 9781600610707

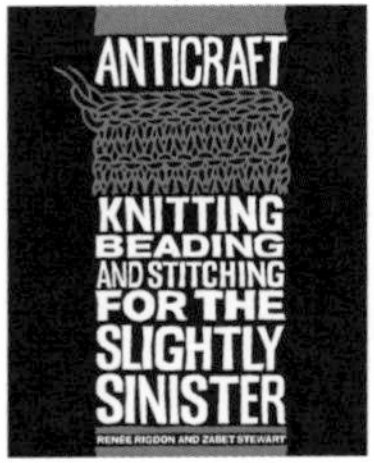
ANTICRAFT
KNITTING
BEADING
AND STITCHING
FOR THE
SLIGHTLY
SINISTER

ANTICRAFT
By Renee Rigdon and Zabet Stewart

Paperback

#Z1356

ISBN: 9781600610301

Seeking Dead People?

Visit **<www.familytreemagazine.com>** for tips and tools to trace your dearly departed ancestors.
Sign up for our e-mail newsletter and get a free digital issue of *Family Tree Magazine*!